The MBTI as a key to congregational dynamics

How We Belong, Fight, and Pray

LLOYD EDWARDS

an alban institute publication

The Publications Program of The Alban Institute is assisted by a grant from Trinity Church, New York City.

Library of Congress Catalog Card Number 93-71924
ISBN 1-56699-114-5

CONTENTS

ACKNOWLEDGMENTS

It is a pleasure to acknowledge the suggestions and encouragement of Celia Allison Hahn and the Rev. John Ackerman.

CHAPTER I

What Do They Need?

When Harry Met Sally

When Harry Wosniak met Sally Reynolds, their friends told them that they were as different as their film counterparts. Harry was spontaneous, while Sally liked to plan her days and follow her plan. Sally had deep sensitivity to her friends' feelings, while Harry approached decisions in a cool, analytic way that sometimes neglected consideration of the feelings of others. Harry liked to travel, liked talking with people, liked keeping up with what was happening in the world in politics, in sports, in every area of life. Sally had fewer interests but seemed to go into them more deeply; she had fewer friends than Harry, but hers were life-long. Sometimes Harry's pace exhausted her; a few hours of quiet time alone recharged her batteries quite nicely.

They were a perfect match. Sally's grandmother said of them, "Well, opposites attract, you know," with such a definitive nod of her head that no one thought otherwise.

After the wedding, they spent a year settling into a satisfying life together. What had initially attracted them to each other grew even more fascinating, so that, as Harry put it once, there was something almost spiritual in their marriage.

When Sally became pregnant, they began looking for a church. Sally had grown up Methodist, Harry Catholic. They talked about what they wanted in a church and decided to compromise on the Episcopal Church, if they could find a congregation they liked.

There was the rub. They gave it a good try. They attended the old downtown parish for a couple of months; they attended a busy suburban parish near where they lived for about three months; they attended a charismatic mission church once; an Anglican high church for three Sundays; and several others for varying periods.

None was quite right for them. At first they would talk about what they didn't like in terms of the looks of the building, the personalities of the clergy, the quality of the programs—especially the nursery and early childhood education programs. But as they kept visiting and talking about their experience, those things seemed less important than their own preferences.

If the worship was spontaneous enough for Harry, it wasn't structured enough for Sally. When she was comfortable because she knew what to expect, he was bored with the sameness of worship week after week. When he was comfortable "going with the flow" in more spontaneous worship, she was uncomfortable and embarrassed because she didn't know how to behave.

Harry generally didn't like the sermons. They seemed to appeal mostly to emotions, and he came away unsatisfied, hungry for clarity and logic. Sally liked the sermons more than Harry but didn't want to defend them to him; after all, his logical criticism was hard to refute and, in their rare arguments, Harry's logic felt cold and uncaring to her.

The baby was born, a beautiful girl. And after almost a year of serious congregational visiting, Harry and Sally and their new daughter are as far from finding a congregational home as they ever were.

What went wrong?

In this book I present a way of understanding congregational life that helps us understand what went wrong with Harry and Sally's search and also how things can go right. This way of looking at a congregation can help us understand many of the conflicts that take place in the congregation, especially conflicts that don't seem to have anything to do with their ostensible subject. It can help us understand some predictable crises in the life of newcomers such as Harry and Sally and can help us make the negotiation of these crises easier. And it can help us understand the various spiritualities present in the congregation.

It can also help us understand some actions that congregational leadership can take to make a congregation a more attractive place for different types of people and the importance of doing that.

This way of understanding is based directly on the ideas developed by Katherine Briggs and her daughter, Isabel Briggs Myers, and independently by the Swiss psychiatrist C.G. Jung. These ideas are primarily known through the Myers-Briggs Type Indicator (MBTI), perhaps the most widely used personality type questionnaire available today. The MBTI is used to obtain information from an individual to help that individual understand his or her psychological type.

I will use the information contained in the MBTI freely, for it is available in many sources, but familiarity or experience with the questionnaire will not be necessary for understanding this book.

While I will describe the elements of the MBTI and use the underlying ideas extensively and freely, I will be using it in a context for which it was not originally intended, i.e., to understand some characteristics of the collective known as the congregation. Nevertheless, I think this use is justified, for I will use it to describe characteristics common to a group of individuals within the congregation, characteristics usually accepted by the individuals as adequately self-describing.

The real validity of this approach is gauged by this question: Is it useful? There are many ways of understanding congregational life, and I only propose that this is a useful one because it helps us understand some things that other approaches necessarily omit.

No new research is presented here. I believe that all the necessary information—the MBTI "lore"—is widely known and that what is missing is the application to the life of a congregation in a way consistent with the intent and limitations of the MBTI.

There are four chapters in this book. Chapter I lays out the elements of the Myers-Briggs-Jung theory and proposes a way to apply it to congregational life. Subsequent chapters deal with conflicts, incorporation and evangelism, and spirituality. An appendix contains a checklist that summarizes many of the ideas.

The reader who is not interested in the various contributions of Myers and Briggs and Jung to the development of the MBTI is invited to skip to the section of this chapter titled "MBTI" for a discussion of the ideas that are important for understanding the remainder of the book.

Briggs and Myers

The MBTI had *its* origins in the origins of Isabel Briggs Myers. She was the daughter of Lyman Briggs, a physicist who at one time directed the National Bureau of Standards, and Katharine Cooke Briggs. Katharine Briggs's father was on the faculty of Michigan State when it was Michigan Agricultural College, and like most faculty children, Katharine Cooke Briggs was tutored at home. It was therefore natural for her to tutor her own children at home, and so Isabel Briggs had little other schooling until her entrance into Swarthmore College, from which she graduated in 1919 with highest honors in political science. From her mother, Isabel Briggs Myers learned that she "could do things without formally studying them" (Lawrence 1988, 5). From her researcher father, she learned that "the greatest fun in the world was to find out something that nobody knew yet, and maybe you could dig it out" (Lawrence 1988, 5 of Ch. 2). Both contributed to her life-long zeal for understanding psychological types.

When Isabel Briggs brought her boyfriend, Clarence G. Myers, home to meet her parents, her mother noted that while he was a remarkable young man, he was not like others in the family. The year was 1917. Mrs. Briggs began reading biographies with the purpose of understanding the differences between people (a remarkable maternal response!). Over the next several years she developed her own theory of types based on her reading and interviews with friends and strangers. She identified meditative types, spontaneous types, executive types, and sociable types (later identified in MBTI terms as I's, EP's, ETJ's and EFJ's).

Isabel Briggs and Clarence Myers were married in 1918, and mother and daughter continued their avid type-watching together for the next eighteen years. A turning point in the development of their ideas occurred in 1923, with the publication in English of Carl G. Jung's *Psychological Types* (1923). In his book Jung proposed a theory of psychological type (described below) based on his reading of myth, drama, and fiction and rooted in his theory of the unconscious. Mrs. Briggs discovered that her theory was quite consistent with his and that, although there was considerable overlap, each had features that the other lacked. She destroyed her own notes (for which Jung later chided her) and began to master every detail of Jung's book. Her work on typology was published in the *New Republic* Magazine on December 26, 1926.

With the outbreak of the Second World War, Isabel Briggs Myers saw in the study of typology a way to help people understand rather than destroy each other. More practically, she saw people volunteering out of patriotism for jobs for which they were not temperamentally suited. She saw that, to be useful, typology must be put on a practical basis. A pencil-and-paper questionnaire, a *type indicator,* was needed.

With single-minded industry, Isabel Briggs Myers threw herself into the development of a questionnaire. Over the next twenty years, using data gathered from friends and strangers, she developed questions that would distinguish among types. Along with her theoretical work, she tested more than 5000 medical students, analyzing dropouts and over- and under-achievers, testing them years later to see if they had chosen specialties that fit their type. They had. She also tested more than 10,000 nursing students.

In time, her work came to the attention of the Educational Testing Service. ETS purchased the rights to the MBTI in 1956, and because of its developer's lack of formal training in psychological testing, also formed the Office of Special Testing to carry on further research on the MBTI. During this time, the MBTI went through a number of different forms. From 1962 until 1975, when the MBTI was acquired by Consulting Psychologists Press, it was available through ETS for research purposes only.

In 1975 the Center for Application for Psychological Type formally came into existence. Located in Gainesville, Florida, it was formerly the Typology Lab at The University of Florida. The Center has led and coordinated research on type using the MBTI.

In 1979 the Association for Psychological Type was formed. It is a membership group composed of professionals from a variety of fields "who seek to extend the development, research, and applications of psychological type theory and the Myers-Briggs Type Indicator." The APT publishes the *Journal of Psychological Type*, a national research journal on the MBTI, and sponsors training events.

In 1980, Isabel Briggs Myers' book *Gifts Differing* was published. She took her title from the Epistle of Paul to the Romans: "For as we have many members in one body, and all members have not the same office, so we, being many, are one body . . . and every one members one of another. Having then gifts differing, let us use them in accordance with the grace that God has given us" (Romans 12:4-8). Like Paul, Mrs.

Myers understood the various types as gifts from God, all valuable, all to be cherished. She saw a distinct value in each of the types and believed that each type made a unique contribution to society. She believed in the usefulness of typology for understanding communications among people and believed strongly in the "mutual usefulness of the opposite types." Her book is not only a valuable introduction to her work, but a testimony to the power of her mind, capable both of analytic rigor and the deepest intuitive insight.

In the same year that her book was published, Isabel Briggs Myers died peacefully in her sleep.

There is some confusion about the name of the MBTI. In a 1973 seminar (Briggs 1973), Isabel Briggs Myers explained that it was originally named the Briggs Myers Type Indicator, listing the primary researcher, her mother, first. But when people looked at her name, they would often think it was simply named for her and would gratuitously insert a hyphen. To make it clear that it was a joint venture, Mrs. Myers reversed the order to give it its present name, the Myers-Briggs Type Indicator. And so it stands.

Jung

The outline of Jung's life and thought is now quite well known (Hall 1973). Most explanations of the MBTI do not set his ideas in the context of his seminal work on the psyche. In this section I will do that. Jung's description of his typology is not the last word, however, and we will come back to a more nuanced description in the section titled "MBTI."

Jung's greatest idea, and the foundation of all his other ideas, is the objective existence and autonomy of the psyche. Initially he was much like the physicists of the past centuries who had a great deal of data, but lacked the concept of the electron, with its specific characteristics, to organize and explain the data. There was a great deal of data which, in Jung's retrospect, called for the concept of the psyche to provide the basis for a satisfactory explanation. Because no one has seen either an electron or a psyche, the gathering of data to support the existence of these entities is inevitably indirect. Once the concept is proposed, however, and is seen to explain the data, the concept takes on a certain reality. Now people speak matter-of-factly of electrons, and many speak so of the psyche.

It is interesting that the characteristics of electrons have undergone distinct changes in order to explain new data suggested by new theories. People still accept the electron as "real" despite these changes. Perhaps the psyche is similar; originally an abstract hypothesis, it has taken on more and more reality. It may change its characteristics somewhat to meet the demands of new theories, but its "reality" will not be given up by those who accept it.

What is the evidence for the existence of the psyche? Jung's interest probably began in childhood with his awareness of his own dreams and his mother's psychic abilities. Later his fascination with psychic phenomena in his family (a loud crack from the sideboard with no apparent cause, a vigorously ringing doorbell with no ringer, a series of seances) and his discovery that similar psychic phenomena had been recorded around the world led him to propose the existence of an entity that created them. His studies with Freud and others gave more data—self-disclosing slips of the tongue and pauses in word-associations—which led to the discovery of complexes, of the unconscious, and then of the collective unconscious.

Where do these come from? From the psyche, said Jung, and he proceeded to catalog its contents. The psyche is composed of three components: consciousness, the personal unconscious, and the collective unconscious. The contents of consciousness are sense perceptions, which tell us *that* something is, but not *what* it is; thinking, which tells us *what* it is; feeling, which is the emotional indicator of evaluation (I like this, don't like that; this is beautiful, etc.); intuition, which tells the possibilities inherent in the situation; volitional processes, which are under the control of the will; instinctual processes, which are characterized by freedom and compulsiveness; and dreams. The Feeling and Thinking functions Jung called judging functions, for they are alternate ways of making judgments. The Sensing and iNtuiting functions he called perceptive functions, for they are alternative ways of perceiving. To complete the catalogue of the contents of the psyche, the unconscious contains both those contents which were once conscious to the individual or which could have been conscious to the individual had they been sufficiently important (personal unconscious) and those contents which were never even potentially conscious to the individual (collective unconscious).

When Jung claimed the objective existence and autonomy of the psyche, he meant, first, that it existed as an object and could therefore be an object of study and research. There is something real there, he claimed; it can be studied, and it will explain the appropriate empirical data.

Further, he meant that the psyche was not derivative from some other branch of knowledge: "Psychology is neither biology nor physiology nor any other science than just this knowledge of the psyche" (Jung 1923, 30). Jung thereby laid the basis for the study of psychology as a science in itself, independent of other sciences; with one blow he severed both psychology's dependence on other sciences and its dependence on the materialism so dear to Freud.

Jung described the psyche as a system of psychic energy, which he called libido. It is more or less self-contained and relatively stable. It receives energy continuously from the outer world through the senses and therefore can never come to complete equilibrium but in its healthiest state exists between the extremes of complete openness, or chaos, and complete closedness, or stagnation (Hall 1973).

With this background, we can turn to Jung's description of attitudes and functions of the psyche. The attitude-types are called *Extraverted* and *Introverted.* They are distinguished by the direction of movement of psychic energy. The Introvert internalizes the object, then receives energy from his or her internal representation of the object, as if to prevent the object itself from gaining power over him. The Extravert gives attention to the object, affirming its importance; the object becomes so important that it influences his subjective attitude, and he receives energy from the object itself. "Everyone knows reserved, inscrutable, rather shy people who form the strongest possible contrast to the open, sociable, jovial or at least friendly and approachable characters who are on good terms with everybody, or quarrel with everybody, but always relate to them in some way and in turn are affected by them" (Campbell 1971, 179, excerpted from Jung's *Psychological Types*). Thus Jung described the attitude-types. They are fundamental psychological distinctions, and Jung characteristically describes the extremes as sharp dichotomies. In a more nuanced description, such as in the MBTI description, we find a continuum of types, with Jung's descriptions at the extremes and with attention paid to the important auxiliary functions.

The functions of the psyche, what the psyche *does*, are important. They are listed earlier as psychic contents: Thinking, Feeling, iNtuiting, and Sensing.

The functions come in pairs. Thinking and Feeling are one pair, Sensing and iNtuition another. They are complementary pairs in the sense that the psyche cannot do both things simultaneously. They are like a dual tool, say a shovel and pickaxe, with a single shared handle.

The functions are partly conscious and partly unconscious. Very early in life one function distinguishes itself by being more conscious than the others. It is called the *dominant* function. Its complementary function, the *inferior* function, is less conscious than the others. For instance, if the Thinking function is superior, then the Feeling function will be the inferior one.

The more conscious of the other pair is the *auxiliary*; the less conscious of the other pair is usually unnamed.

For a function to be relatively conscious, it is dependable and differentiated compared with less conscious functions. It is used more, it is more trustworthy, it is more refined, capable of more delicacy and subtlety.

Similarly, a relatively unconscious function is less dependable. Sometimes it works well, but it is not under control of the ego. It is less refined, less subtle. An inferior Thinking function, for example, will not be as capable of discriminating, refined distinctions as a superior Thinking function. An inferior Feeling function may flood the person with ill-timed and embarrassing emotion, where a superior Feeling function will be more capable of finely discriminated values distinctions.

It is a mistake to say, for instance, that if my inferior function is Thinking, that I don't think as much; rather my preference for Thinking is less, my preference for Feeling is greater (in making decisions). The nature of my thinking will be different from that of someone whose Thinking is her superior function.

It is surprising that Jung's psychological typology is relatively neglected among Jungians.[1] Perhaps it is because it is one of the less controversial of his proposals; perhaps it is because it is less directly important for the practice of analysis than other ideas. And perhaps it is that, without a type indicator, the ideas of typology are less useful than others.

Whatever the reason, it remained for Myers and Briggs to make the necessary final additions to the theory and to publish the type indicator, which has disseminated Jung's thoughts so widely.

The MBTI

Jung's theory was a milestone in psychological understanding, but it was not without its faults. For one thing, it described the different types in the sharpest, most extreme terms. As he pointed out, his descriptions fit virtually no real persons, because most real persons do not fit the descriptions of "pure types" which Jung provided.

Real persons also have auxiliary functions, the more-conscious functions of the other pair. The auxiliary is always present and moderates the effects of the dominant process.

Jung's descriptions of the Introverted types suffer from his own stereotypes and would probably not be accepted by anyone who is very introverted. He also neglected to draw out the implications of his insight, i.e., that the auxiliary function is oppositely directed from the dominant. For example, if the person is Introverted iNtuitive, her auxiliary, whether it is Thinking or Feeling, will be Extraverted. These defects were remedied by Myers in her work on the MBTI.

The MBTI is a pencil-and-paper questionnaire that elicits the preferences of an individual on four scales. The scales may be thought of as straight line continua with extremes at the end. The scales are labeled with the extremes.

The first scale is the *Extraversion-Introversion* scale. It describes where one prefers to focus one's attention: to the outer or the inner world. People with Extravert preference have a positive relation to people, places, and things of the outer world. They receive energy, stimulation, from things of the outer world, and they imbue them with interest and importance: people, crowds, events, things happening, movement.

Those with Introvert preference prefer things of the inner world: ideas, feelings, intuitions. They draw energy from these things, while external things drain them of energy.

If an Extravert and an Introvert go to a party, the Extravert is more likely to talk briefly with a lot of people, stay later, and go home energized, so that he wants to talk about the party to wind down. The Introvert is more likely to enjoy talking in a small group or with one person at a time, go home drained of energy, and need some time alone to regain her energy.

These are descriptions of people with strong preferences; they would place themselves on the ends of the scale. Most people are nearer the middle, and so it is not strictly accurate to say that we are Introverted or Extraverted. We can relate to the outer world or to the inner world, but we usually have a clear preference for one over the other. When we say for brevity that someone is an Introvert, we mean that they have a preference for Introversion over Extraversion, but they still have some preference for Extraversion, at least on occasion.

There are other differences between Introverts and Extraverts. Extraverts usually prefer to communicate by talking; Introverts by writing. Introverts find out what they think by going inside themselves; this process is rather slow compared with the Extravert's process, but the result is usually a more refined, nuanced statement. Extraverts find out what they think by talking about it; their reflective process is faster and more public, but their "final statement" may not be as final as it sounds. Extraverts tend to act first, then (perhaps) to reflect, while Introverts tend to reflect first, then (perhaps) to act.

Suppose that an Introvert and an Extravert have just seen the same film and you ask them how they likedit. The Extravert will probably want to talk about it and will be quicker to offer an opinion. The Extravert's opinion may change in the course of the conversation. The Introvert may not want to commit to an opinion right away, perhaps not until the next morning, and will need to think it through before answering.

Extraverts tend to prefer to work around other people and like input from others. Introverts prefer to work quietly alone and find interruptions distracting.

The second scale is the *Sensing-iNtuiting* scale. Because "I" has already been used for Introvert, INtuition is abbreviated by "N", so this scale is usually called the S-N scale.

The S-N scale describes how we take in information. People with a strong Sensing preference take in information through the senses: tasting, seeing, touching, hearing, smelling. They are "in touch with what's there." People with a strong iNtuition preference take in information through a "sixth sense" or hunch. They trust their "gut feelings" for information. They take in information indirectly and find patterns or possibilities in what they see and hear.

One way to try to understand the iNtuition is that it synthesizes the immense amount of sensory data that the psyche receives unconsciously and then presents it to awareness. This interpretation, while attractive, is not part of either the Jungian nor the Myers-Briggs lore about the iNtuitive function.

If two people, one with a strong Sensing preference and the other with a strong iNtuiting preference, entered a room, stayed a few minutes, and left, they would have quite different information about the room. The Sensing type would likely remember the details of the room: the patterns of the upholstery, the contents of the pictures on the walls, the colors of the wallpaper, the names of the periodicals on the coffee table. The iNtuiting type would be unlikely to remember that kind of detail. These are complementary functions, and the iNtuiting type would rather take in information about patterns and possibilities: what might be done with the room by a decorator, what the room has been used for, and even what kinds of people have used it. The iNtuitive would be as confident of his information as the Sensing type is of hers.

When I was a child I read childrens' magazines that often contained a particular kind of game. The reader was shown a picture of a room containing many objects. The instructions were to look at the picture for one minute, then cover it and try to list as many of the objects in the picture as possible. It was a test of sensing ability and sensate memory. Sensing types might be expected to do well; iNtuitive types might be expected to do poorly by comparison.

There are other characteristic differences between the Sensing and iNtuitive types. Sensing types are more practical-minded than iNtuitives, while iNtuitives are more innovative than Sensing types. INtuitives prefer to deal with possibilities, while Sensing types prefer to deal with concrete matters, with what's here and now. Sensing types handle detail and routine better than iNtuitives. They seldom make errors of fact and prefer to use established routines to accomplish their tasks. They learn best by starting at the beginning and going step-by-step through the details of the material. INtuitives prefer learning something new or doing something familiar in a new way. They are patient with complexity, but may overlook details. They learn best by getting the big picture and working down to the details (but in class may lose interest before the teacher gets to the details). INtuitive types tend to score better on standardized tests because they are more comfortable working with ambiguous symbols; Sensing types score better on tests of fact and accuracy.

The third scale is the *Thinking-Feeling* scale. It describes characteristic ways that people make decisions. People who have a preference for

Thinking make rational-logical decisions, while people who have a preference for Feeling make decisions based on deeply held values. Both are good ways to make decisions; those who use Thinking generally find that Thinking works well for them, while those who prefer Feeling generally find that Feeling works well for them.

Many people have less clear preferences for Thinking or Feeling. They find themselves somewhere closer to the middle of the T-F scale than to the ends. When it comes to making decisions, they often find themselves torn between the demands of Thinking and Feeling, or between head and heart. Knowledge of typology doesn't help much in making decisions, but it does at least label the ambivalence, and it does affirm that both ways are valid.

Notice that feelings have to do with values. The terms are not the most descriptive and may be a bit misleading. Someone with a Feeling preference does not make decisions based on transient emotions, but rather on deeply held values. The emotions are the tip of the values iceberg and serve to let the person know what his or her values are, but it is values, not emotions, that are at stake when a decision is made.

Here are some other characteristic differences between Thinking and Feeling. People with clear preferences for Thinking tend to analyze courses of action and base their analysis on logical consequences. They make decisions objectively, on the basis of cause-and-effect. They are not afraid of facing upleasant facts. They value justice and objectivity and are good at analyzing what is wrong with something. They view the situation from a distance and take the long view.

Those with clear preferences for Feeling (valuing) care about what is important to the people involved and make decisions on the basis of person-centered values. They tend to imagine themselves in the situation and tend to take the immediate, short view. They like dealing with people and tend to be sympathetic, appreciative, and tactful. They value harmony and are often willing to work hard to achieve it.

Feeling types may learn history, for example, through reading biographies of historically important people, while Thinking types may learn better through reading analyses of the decisions those people made.

In making a decision, Thinking types will concentrate on the decision itself and make sure that the facts are truthfully laid out, that sound principles are followed, and that the logic is correct. Feeling types will be more concerned with how and to whom the decision is announced and how it will affect their lives and their harmony.

In work, Thinking types value brevity and fairness. They tend to be better at working with things and ideas than with people.

Feeling types value interactions with others. They tend to be friendly and concerned about the persons they work with and want to be treated as a person with legitimate feelings and needs.

The fourth scale is the *Judgment-Perception* scale. It describes a person's preferences about her or his lifestyle. A person with strong judgment preference will prefer an orderly, planned lifestyle, whereas a person with strong perception preference prefers a more spontaneous, go-with-the-flow lifestyle.

Again, the terms are not very descriptive. They come from Jung's classification of the Thinking and Feeling functions as judging functions and the Sensing-iNtuiting functions as perceiving functions. That classification is not used in MBTI, and so Judging and Perceiving are simply labels for the fourth scale. In particular, "judging" does not mean being judgmental or condemning.

The J-P preference is often especially important in counseling with couples. Jerry and Betty went to their counselor saying that they couldn't plan and do anything together and that it had become a problem for them. In talking with them, the counselor learned that Jerry had a time-management calendar that was divided into fifteen-minute intervals. His practice was to sit down on Sunday evening and plan his whole week in fifteen-minute intervals. He would ask Betty, "Would you like to play tennis next Saturday between 10 a.m. and 12 noon?" Betty preferred a more spontaneous lifestyle and did not like to be "planned in" like that. She would typically say to Jerry, "Ask me at 10 a.m. next Saturday," to which Jerry would reply, "But I need to know *now* so I can plan my time!" Both held responsible jobs, and both of their ways of managing their time worked well for them in their jobs. It was only when they tried to plan something together that they had problems.

In counseling two things happened. First, each began to recognize what the other brought to their life. Jerry brought Betty some structure which, within limits, felt good to her. Betty brought Jerry some spontaneity which, within limits, was fun for him.

They also began to learn to compromise. She said, "I'll play tennis with you between 10 and 12, but don't plan me in any other time!" And he said, "I'll block out 4 to 6 p.m. to be spontaneous with you, but that's about as much spontaneity as I can take." And of course they lived happily ever after, as people in examples do.

Linda is a consultant in a high-stress environment. She had always assumed that being a J was good and that there was something wrong with her because she wasn't. After she found that her true preference was strongly P, she re-organized her office. She recognized her preference for putting on a high-energy "push" just before an important presentation—which she had previously condemned in herself as "leaving things 'til the last minute"—and notified her staff to expect it and to plan their time around it. She is working more effectively and her work is much less stressful to her as a result of the changes she has made.

Here are some other characteristic differences between Judging and Perceiving. People with a strong J preference like to make decisions and move ahead. They like to plan and are naturally more comfortable when they exert considerable control over the events around them. They prefer structure and organization and generally do not like ambiguity.

People with a strong P preference like to live in a flexible, spontaneous way. They want to keep their options open because there might be new information that would affect their decision. They prefer to understand life rather than control it.

Those who take the MBTI receive their results in the form of four pairs of numbers. The first pair expresses the preference strengths of the E-I pair, the second of the S-N pair, etc. Taking the strongest preference of each pair, one can form the person's *psychological type* as presented by the MBTI.

Because there are four scales with two pairs of preferences for each scale, there are sixteen psychological types. The types are labeled with the four highest-scored preferences: INFP, ESTJ, etc. The sixteen psychological types are often displayed in a four-by-four *type table.*

The frequencies of occurrence of the different preferences and of the psychological types are important. Particular samples, such as medical school classes, have been studied extensively (Myers 1980). Of necessity the statistics for the "general population" are less accurate. These numbers, taken from Lawrence (1982), are intended to be indicative, but they are important for understanding some of the dynamics of a congregation.

The frequency of occurrence of Extraverts and Introverts is approximately seventy-five percent to twenty-five percent. People who prefer Sensing outnumber those who prefer iNtuiting by the same proportion, approximately seventy-five percent to twenty-five percent. Both these figures are independent of gender. On the Thinking-Feeling scale, gender plays a role. The ratio of those who prefer Thinking to Feeling is roughly sixty percent to forty percent for men, while it is reversed, roughly forty percent to sixty percent, for women. Finally, the ratio of those who prefer Judgment to Perception is about fifty-five percent to forty-five percent.

There are important implications to be drawn from these percentages. For example, Extraverted-Sensing preferences, which appear in only twenty-five percent (four of sixteen) of the MBTI types, represent fifty-six percent of the population! Introverted-iNtuitive types, which also represent twenty-five percent of the MBTI types, represent only six percent of the population.

Many Introverted iNtuitives report that they grew up feeling strange, as if the institutions that taught and shaped them discriminated against them. And there is truth to this observation. Institutions such as schools tend to reward the majority, and certain types are in the distinct minority. The book *People Types and Tiger Stripes* (Lawrence 1982) was written to help teachers to teach the various types appropriately, but these ideas have a long way to go before they enter the educational mainstream in American schools. Nonetheless, it is true that "the appreciation of the normality of Introversion by Jungian psychology is a kind of Introverts-Lib movement" (Wilmer 1987, 157).

We will not use the type table to any extent, nor even the sixteen psychological types. Our interest will be with the four pairs of preferences and their occurrence in the congregation.

Temperaments

We will also use a simplified view of type, called temperament, proposed in Kiersey (1978). Kiersey and Bates propose four temperaments, labeled SJ, NT, SP, and NF. Here is a very brief description of each.

The SJs bring order and stability to the institutions to which they belong; they are stabilizers. They like traditional ways of doing things and are usually willing to devote a great deal of time and energy to making sure that institutions function well. They are loyal to their institutions, whether church, family, or nation, and take on the necessary concrete, week-to-week tasks necessary for the successful institutional life, doing them with perseverance and patience. They are thorough, hard-working, and set and meet high standards for themselves. They prefer to follow a plan and value duty highly. They tend to expect the same of others. If they have a flaw, it is their failure to deal with the significance of changing times.

The NTs are visionaries, going for new ideas and new projects with boldness and independence. They are forward-looking and are stimulating and challenging to work with. Change is no problem for them; rather they often chafe at others' resistance to change, and they do not do repetitive or illogical tasks gladly. They need freedom to work their ideas independently of others and value being appreciated for their intellectual competence and ingenuity.

The SPs function best when there is a crisis, for they are natural troubleshooters. They like action and drama and do best when there is a practical, hands-on, short-term task to be done. They are easily bored with routine and look for ways to make their lives and the lives of others more exciting. They are often good risk-takers.

The NFs are the catalysts or connectors in the organization. They are usually warm, informal, and personal, and their gift is to keep everyone working well together by appreciating each person's special gifts. They are enthusiastic and empathetic and work best when they receive personal, affirming feedback. They may burn out quicker than other temperaments by trying to be too helpful.

What do they need?

In *The Magic Monastery*, Theophane the Monk tells the following story.

> There's a monk there who will never give you advice, but only a question. I was told his questions could be very helpful. I sought him out. "I am a parish priest," I said. "I'm here on retreat. Could you give me a question?"
>
> "Ah, yes," he answered. "My question is, 'What do they need?'"
>
> I came away disappointed. I spent a few hours with the question, writing out answers, but finally I went back to him.
>
> "Excuse me. Perhaps I didn't make myself clear. Your

question has been helpful, but I wasn't so much interested in thinking about my apostolate during this retreat. Rather I wanted to think seriously about my own spiritual life. Could you give me a question for my own spiritual life?"

"Ah, I see. Then my question is, 'What do they REALLY need?'"

Tales of a Magic Monastery by Theophane the Monk.

Theophane's story raises many questions—questions of co-dependency in the parish, of the difference between what parishioners want and what they need, of whether the parish priest is the primary (read "only real") pastoral minister, and others. Nonetheless, it does focus my contention in this book: that any congregation is composed of people with different typologies and therefore with different preferences; that they need quite different things in the congregational environment in order to function well as congregational members; that most of the people in any congregation are unsophisticated about typology and don't know what their particular typologically-based needs are; and that the congregational leadership can and should go a long way toward ensuring that these basic environmental needs are met.

There are several assumptions underlying this contention: that typology is valid and significant as a description of groups of people in the congregation; that different types or preferences are equally valuable, as Jung, Myers, Briggs, and many other writers affirm; and that an "all-type-friendly" congregation is desirable and possible.

Much of the value of the MBTI lies in the fact that people nearly always accept it as a valid self-description. My experience is that people who take the MBTI usually find it a surprisingly accurate description of themselves, and it is couched in terms that they accept as valid for themselves. They not only accept the descriptions as mostly accurate for themselves, but see the common characteristics between themselves and others of similar type. That is unusual for a set of psychological categories, especially when many people are originally cautious about "being put in a box." Because people generally accept the descriptions as applicable to themselves, even to the point of identifying themselves with the descriptions, it seems valid to apply those descriptions to groups of people in the parish, provided that the characteristics attributed to the groups do not go farther than those of the MBTI itself.

The equal validity of different types in the congregation is deceptively acceptable. Before an easy "of course they are" is given, the reader is invited to read the rest of this book to see some of the implications of that assumption. It may be easy to accept in principle, but the price to be paid for the implementation may be high.

The same is true for the desirability for an "all-type-friendly" congregation. Questions may arise such as: Do we really want to give up our identity as a congregation or as a denomination (based on the preponderance of one or a few types) in order to accept people different from ourselves? The answer from experience is often "no" when the differences are cultural or economic. It is not obvious that the answer is different when the differences are typological.

In fact it could be argued that one of the reasons for the existence of denominations is to provide a comfortable type-similar setting for particular types of people. It is an amusing parlor game to propose, for example, that the Episcopalians are predominantly INF, the Southern Baptists ES, the Lutherans INT, etc. To my knowledge no research has been done to support or deny these conjectures. (William Bridges has written a book on describing the corporate type of an organization [1992]). Yet denominations *do* have identities or personalities, and if type *is* a significant part of such a description, the value of an "all-type-friendly" congregation would be in direct conflict with the value of the congregational identity.

Yet I believe that such an awareness in a congregation is not only desirable but crucial for the church and for the world now. I believe that our most pressing need is to learn to get along with people who are different from ourselves—not just to tolerate them, and not to deny the differences, but to value and celebrate the differences. We have for too long flocked together with folks like us and then ministered to those who are unlike us in order to help them become like us. The congregation must become a laboratory for learning to live with those who are different from us and to appreciate the differences. I believe that this is the church's current challenge, its current quest on the journey to the Kingdom of God. Our biggest deterrent is the chauvinistic idea that everyone is really just like me, with the same ways of seeing the world, the same ways of making decisions, the same assumptions about what is right and wrong, and the same spiritual needs—and that if they're different from me, there is something wrong with them. To realize that there really are people different from us can be frightening and disorienting, as well as salutary. The MBTI can help us with this shock of recognition.

An exercise: Imagine that you are standing on the rim of the Grand Canyon with your best friend. What do you see? Now imagine that your friend begins to describe what he or she sees and that it is *quite* different from your description! What would you think? How would that feel to you?

If some version of "either my friend is crazy or I am" came to mind, you can understand some of the fear and disorientation that true recognition of differences can bring. Usually we can agree on what objects we see (although we can never be sure that the colors I see are the same as the ones you see; there is always the residue of subjectivity, even in describing objects). But even when we see the same objects, the *meaning* of the objects may be quite different for different people.

Another exercise: In your congregation, pay attention to who remembers whose names (and to whose names you remember). Do men tend to remember men's names and forget women's names? Do women tend to remember women's names and forget men's names?

I believe that that is true and that it is based on something deeper than the vicissitudes of memory. When men look at a scene, they notice men and do not notice women; they pay more attention to men's activities and less to women's activities. And the same is true with women. They notice and remember other women and their activities more and they notice and remember men and their activities less.

If this is true, as I believe, then men and women, looking at the same scene, see different scenes. Different things count as important for them; different aspects of the scene come to the psychological foreground and others recede to the background. Even when men and women talk about a shared experience, they are describing different personal experiences, different realities. The differences may seem slight, but they are quite significant. The effort required to imagine the other person's reality can be very great, and the success at doing so is usually limited.

This is both an example and a metaphor for the kind of work that the MBTI demands: the imaginative effort to empathetically understand the other person's point of view; the jarring realization that there really are people who perceive, think, etc., in ways distinctly different from mine; the failure finally to *understand* the differences; and finally the ability to trust the other person's perceptions, feelings, etc., despite one's inability to understand them.

The body of Christ has a voice, and it is the voices of all the members of the congregation. They must all be spoken and heard by each other! The Extraverts must be listened to and not pinned down to their final word; the Introverts must be asked again and again. When all the voices are heard and cherished, when the differences are appreciated and truly valued, the Kingdom will have come very near!

The remainder of this book is a reflection on the question, "What do they need?" What are the legitimate needs of the various psychological types? How can we be wise enough to understand those needs and to attempt to meet them in the congregation? What are the implications of an "all-type-friendly" congregation?

If we accept the differences between people as legitimate, we must also accept the inevitability of conflict—not conflicts as problems to be solved, but conflict as a way of life. I don't mean to imply hostility by the term conflict but rather the realization of significant differences, differences that don't go away with a bit of persuasion or coercion. Chapter II reflects on inevitable conflicts in the congregation and how to understand and live with them.

The incorporation of newcomers is an important part of the life of the congregation. Some years ago Will Shutz proposed the ICA theory, which describes how some primary needs of group members—Inclusion, Control, and Affective expression—are met in their group. The ICA theory combines nicely with the MBTI to help us understand some of the challenges faced by newcomers and also gives us some clues as to effective evangelism. That is the subject of Chapter III.

Congregational spirituality should be one of the central issues in any psychological description of the congregation. You may have raised red flags about the use of psychological description in this book, fearing that transcendence will be reduced to psychological or transpersonal transcendence. I will not make that error, but avoiding it requires careful discrimination. Spirituality in the congregation is the topic of Chapter IV.

Finally, the results of all these reflections are gathered into the appendix in a checklist. It is meant to be as practical as possible, something you can carry in your hand as you walk around the building, something you can take into a meeting and discuss, something you can easily convert into a questionnaire and distribute. It is not a "congregational

MBTI," to tell you the type of the congregation (for that would wash out the differences) but rather a checklist that helps to affirm the differences by asking, "What do they need? What do I need? Are their and my needs being met? Or are we (unintentionally) screening against certain types of people?"

NOTE

1. For example, Wilmer (1987) devotes thirteen pages of 269 to typology; von Franz (1975), six pages of 286; McGuire (1977), four of 469; and Whitmont (1969), seventeen of 310. This corresponds to my experience in Jungian analysis in which typology played an insignificant role at the conscious level.

CHAPTER II

Predictable Conflicts in the Congregation

The Case of the Messy Desk

The front page headline blared, "City businessman guilty of cover-up in messy desk race" (State 1992). The article told how local businessman George Satterfield had ignored pleas from his family, co-workers, and customers to clean off his desk. "I've never lost a thing," he said. "If I can't find something in a couple of seconds, it's probably not on my desk."

Satterfield was identified as the owner of the messiest desk in the area by Priority Management Systems, a company that sells training programs to help people become better organized and more productive. Ken Morris, an associate of Priority Management Systems, said, "People typically are lazy, or they don't see the value of a clean desk. All that stuff represents unfinished work. People are very insecure about putting it out of sight."

Morris' company offered to give Satterfield a free program. Satterfield says he doesn't need it. He can dig down to find every organizer he's ever tried. They are all still there, and none of them has worked for him.

Norms, Language, and Politics

Clearly it was in Ken Morris' business interests to promote the norm: clean desk is good; messy desk is bad. It helped him to sell his systems. He promoted his norm through an ersatz competition, and the newspaper collaborated with him in his promotion. He reinforced his norm with harsh words: anyone who doesn't conform to his norm is lazy and insecure. He identified Satterfield and held him up to public ridicule to sell systems.

Satterfield's norm was not Morris', and he didn't accept the norm nor the program as his own.

This may seem like a trivial incident, but it is one that occurs every day in every organization, including congregations. Someone uses language to set up a norm. Those who don't measure up to the norm are at least expected to explain why they do not; in extreme cases they are expected to leave the organization.

There is always a payoff, and so norm setting is a political game. In Morris' case the payoff is greater income; usually in congregational life, power is the payoff.

Much norm setting is unconscious. It is the nature of people to believe that their opinions, their values, their ways of doing things are the right ones and that those who disagree, hold different values, or do things differently are wrong. The norms are assumed and unquestioned. The hoped-for payoff is a feeling of natural superiority, of being special, of being right.

Whether it is unconscious or not, this kind of norming is often destructive of community in the larger sense. Episcopal Presiding Bishop Edmond Browning once said that he spent most of his time trying to keep some group in the church from running some other group out of the church. He has taken as one of the marks of his tenure as Presiding Bishop the phrase "no outcasts." The MBTI helps us see how difficult it is to uphold that value in practice.

There are all kinds of conflicts in congregations and in the larger church. Some are healthy, open conflicts; the issues are clear and pretty much agreed upon by both sides; there doesn't seem to be a need to personalize the conflict. In these conflicts, people don't feel that their identity or well-being is at stake.

For example, a congregation undertakes a building program. They engage three architects to present preliminary sketches. The sketches are posted on the wall at the coffee hour and the members choose their preferred sketch. They talk about the differences; they argue about what it will mean for themselves and for the future of the congregation if this one or that one is chosen; they propose changes in the sketches. Out of this can come better ideas and greater satisfaction with the final proposal.

In this kind of conflict the various parties can agree on what the conflict is about. They can understand that someone can disagree with them without being evil or malicious, and they do not necessarily feel that to lose the vote is to lose something vital.

The kind of conflict I want to reflect on here is a different kind, a kind found all too often in congregations today. Here the conflict seems unbalanced. One side sees it as a life-or-death issue, and the other side is hardly aware that there is a conflict. The life-or-death people seem to see their identity at stake and are ready to fight as if for their lives. The other side doesn't see the issue as life-or-death for themselves or for anyone else and doesn't see what the fuss is about. The life-or-death people are angered further because no one takes them seriously, and they are correct in their perception; the other side doesn't understand the depth of their commitment to the issue. But they are unable to say what the issue is in a way that seems compelling to the other side. Thus the conflict is irresolvable within the usual framework, for there is no common ground for discussion.

I believe that there are certain conflicts that are inevitable and that many are of this second type. They arise from our innate differences: differences in the way we relate to the things around us, in the way we perceive reality, in the ways we make decisions, in the ways we choose to live our lives. Often we are unaware of the depth of these conflicts in ourselves or in the other side, so that they can seem vital or trivial, depending on which side we're on. Usually one side does not see the deep importance that the issue holds for the other side and cannot understand why anyone would get so invested in such a trivial issue. Yet if *we* are invested the issue is vitally important, so important that someone cannot challenge us in these areas without threatening us or seeming to attack us.

These conflicts often involve norming and the use of language to exclude and include. We can make a great stride toward understanding them through understanding the MBTI distinctions. Although there are many different ways to understand congregational conflict, the MBTI offers many insights not found in alternative viewpoints.

Types and Conflicts

One of the great virtues of the MBTI is that it does not lend itself easily to this kind of political norming. There are no built-in norms except the norm of acceptability of all types. On the contrary, the values implicit in the MBTI are that all psychological types are of value, despite what society says, and despite their statistical frequency.

From the early days of type development, Myers and Briggs took scrupulous care to make sure that each type would be described in words acceptable to that type. For example, no negative words were allowed. If one type was "planned and orderly," the opposite was not "un-planned" or "dis-orderly;" rather, it was "spontaneous" or "go-with-the-flow." Myers and Briggs realized that using negative words set up norms that implicitly said that one type was preferable to another. This contradicted their belief that all types are valuable.

Despite their care in constructing the type indicator, it is true that opposite types often have low regard for each other. It is part of our instinctive chauvinism that we often affirm our own worth by denying that of someone else. Thus Extraverts say that Introverts are anti-social or withdrawn, while Introverts claim that Extraverts are shallow and superficial; Sensing types claim that iNtuitives are impractical daydreamers, while iNtuitives say that Sensing types are unimaginative and literal-minded; Thinking types may seem cold and condescending to Feeling types, while Feeling types may seem fuzzy-minded and emotional to Thinking types; and Judging types may seem demanding, rigid, and uptight to Perceiving types, while Perceiving types may seem disorganized, messy, and irresponsible to Judging types (Page 1983). While those who are knowledgable about type may affirm the contributions of their opposites, it is also true that in unguarded moments they may succumb to the ancient idea that everything would be better if only everyone perceived, thought, felt, and understood "just as I do."

Congregations, even denominations, are subject to these prejudices. For example, leaders often design programs according to their own preferences and assume that others will find them attractive. It is surprising how often an implicit norm is thus set up, often based on typology. Certain people are supported and affirmed by the norms; the rest are less valued or even excluded.

Even where there is no implicit norm, the MBTI categories are often useful in understanding the inevitable and unresolvable conflicts in a congregation.

Some Examples

Let's go back to Harry and Sally and their search for a congregation. Remember that Harry liked change and spontaneity in the liturgy; Sally liked stability and order. Is this a resolvable conflict? No, it isn't, not when it is understood in those terms.

These are characteristic preferences of two persons, one with a strong preference for Perception (Harry) and the other with a strong preference for Judgment (Sally). They are persistent preferences. They are not open to rational argument. Education will not change their basic preference. Neither one is going to talk the other into the opposite point of view nor should they try to do so. They are going to disagree about these general values forever, and they had better get used to it.

True, they might agree to compromise in a particular, well-defined situation, such as where to go on a particular date or which service to attend on a particular Sunday, but their preferences are strong, clear, and conflicting.

Think of the groups in the congregation that Harry and Sally represent. One group likes spontaneity and change; the other group claims that the first just likes change for its own sake. The second group likes stability and order; the first claims that the second group is mossbacked and unyielding. I have had the experience of greeting people at the church door after the Sunday service and having one person say to me, "Why do we have to do everything the same, Sunday after Sunday?" and the person following say, "Why do we keep changing things every week?"

Is this conflict predictable? Yes, just from the fact that different types are represented in the congregation.

Is it solvable? No and yes. It is not solvable at this level. Such a solution would have winners and losers, and these types are so deeply ingrained that they seem like one's own identity. (Are they "really" one's own identity? I'll come back to this in the chapter on spirituality.) To lose such a conflict would be to feel that there is no place in the church for one's self.

If the conflict can be managed at the specific, pragmatic, problem-solving level, then it is possible that compromises can be reached as the problems arise, so that everyone is equally dissatisfied. As long as the anxiety in the congregation is not too high, it is possible that this will be acceptable to all.

Here is another example of a predictable and never-finally-resolvable conflict. It is taken from the life of my own denomination, but I assume that you can identify a sufficient number of such conflicts in your own to test the usefulness of these ideas.

In the 1970's the Episcopal Church restored the ancient practice of "passing the peace." Prior to that, it was preserved only in the wedding service in the traditional kiss between bride and groom. In the modern version of the Kiss of Peace, the congregation turns to one another during the Holy Eucharist and shakes hands, saying, "The peace of the Lord be always with you," with the response, "And always with you." Many Episcopalians adopted the practice immediately; others still do not participate. Why? This seemingly simple action is fraught with implications for typology.

First, the Sensing-iNtuitive conflict arises because to many people the introduction of the Peace seemed to be "change for change's sake." It was introduced in the context of the revision of the Book of Common Prayer, which also was conflicted with the same issues. Those who liked to try new things seemed to accept it easily, and it *has* been widely accepted throughout the denomination. Those who did not like it not only regarded it as unnecessary and unjustified change, but regarded themselves as having lost the exchange.

Even more importantly, the Introvert-Extravert conflict was raised by this action. According to MBTI lore, those with Extraverted preferences tend to welcome interruptions. They gather energy from what is outside them. So they may not even have thought of the Peace as an interruption in their worship; if they did, it may have been a welcome one. For those with strong Introverted preferences (and there are many in the Episcopal Church) an interruption is not only an intrusion but an unwelcome interruption of their worship of God.

It was believed that educating the people would ease the transition. If they only understood the value of the new prayer book and of the Peace, it was reasoned, they would accept it more easily. A great deal of education *was* offered, and many accepted the changes easily, but there were many for whom no amount of education would suffice; acceptance would require that they give up too much, that they deny too important a part of who they are. No amount of education will be effective in changing people to their opposite type.

For another example, let's visit an adult Bible study class on Easter Sunday. This is a class of men and women in which the teaching chores are rotated among class members in six-week blocks. The current teacher of the class, Neal Thomason, has spent a great deal of time in preparation. He has read the commentaries thoroughly and has even consulted the New Testament professor at the nearby seminary. His research has yielded six interpretations of the Easter story, each logically valid in the perspective in which it is made, and he is presenting them all to the class with equal weight, so that class members may choose from among them the interpretation they prefer. None of the interpretations is historically based.

Sam Jennings is quietly apoplectic in the back row. He doesn't want to make an undignified fuss, but he feels that Neal is leaving out some of the most important considerations. Neal's six interpretations have not been tested against the wisdom of the consensus of historical scholarship, and they are all from modern thinkers who have little regard for the fact of the historic church. In fact, Sam thinks that Neal believes that everything written prior to this century is mistaken, to be corrected by bold and original thinkers of the present century, and there is some truth to Sam's viewpoint. Besides, Sam doesn't like they way Neal runs the class, for Neal has done away with most of the time-honored agenda, including taking roll and reading the minutes of the last meetings. "Takes too much time," said Neal. "We've been doing it that way since I joined this class; there must have been a reason for it," replied Sam.

Nora Franklin is uncomfortable with Neal's presentation but for a different reason. She believes that he is logical at the expense of people's feelings and sensibilities. While she sees some truth in each of the interpretations Neal presents, she also feels that at least four of his interpretations are wrong because, as she put it, "People just don't act like that—and they didn't even back then!" If all the writers Neal is quoting could get together and talk with one another, they could come to agreement. Nora believes that Neal is one of those people who is sometimes logically correct but wrong-headed (or wrong-hearted) and therefore wrong.

Besides, Neal fills the air and the time with ideas, and Nora feels that there is not enough time left to find out how other people feel about the lesson and about other things as well.

Sara Peacock is not paying much attention. She is impatient with the abstract ideas Neal is presenting. "What do they have to do with the Gospel anyway—with helping people?" She has been thinking about the trip to Haiti she will be taking in a few weeks with a judicatory medical missionary team. "Now *there's* the Gospel for you," she thinks, "really doing some good for somebody." All the theories, all the ideas—what do they really matter? Isn't the Gospel about doing good to others and living a moral life? Frankly she's glad that the trip will take her away from the class for a couple of Sundays because it will be during Neal's tenure as teacher.

Who is right? All of them are, and yet they are in conflict about one of the basics of their faith. It is not doctrinal or theological conflict, but a conflict about what is important to include in the process of coming to an understanding of Scripture. Neal Thomason (NT) likes imagination and logic. Sam Jennings (SJ) likes the authoritative weight of tradition and history. Nora Franklin (NF) likes imagination used in relational ways, and Sara Peacock (SP) likes practical, hands-on opportunities for ministry, avoiding speculative theories.

What would be an ideal way for this class to study Scripture? Probably much as they are doing, but with greater type-awareness, so that they could understand why the others are on different wavelengths and could appreciate the differences. Each needs to articulate her or his own point of view and needs to be heard by the others, but no one needs to win; here winning is losing.

The Ordained Leader and the Congregation

The senior clergyperson in a congregation has more opportunity than any other person to set the typological style in a congregation. If she is unaware of the issues raised in this book, she will probably unconsciously set a one-type norm for the congregation and unwillingly screen against those of dissimilar type. The particular values-laden terms in which she describes the Gospel, the models for Christian understanding and behavior which she puts forth in stories, and her own personality set up an unquestionable norm for the congregation. Some may come into conflict with her and leave the congregation ("but you always lose a few people when the new clergyperson comes, don't you?"). Others will find that with all good will they don't understand her sermons, that her proposed programs seem to them to miss the point, that conversations with her are nonmeetings of the mind. They will soon leave, become inactive, or stay and form the loyal opposition.

With awareness comes responsibility. An aware senior clergyperson in a multi-staff congregation can avoid self-replication by hiring assistants of opposite types and by giving them some visibility and support so that people can form relations with them. He can listen to people that he doesn't trust because of their opposite typology (shadow to his own) and can use *their* language to reflect his understanding of their concerns. He can include people of opposite type to his on appointive bodies, not just as a politically astute token act, but in the sincere conviction that a variety of types leads to better decisions. He can monitor the newsletter, bulletin boards, radio broadcasts, etc., for type chauvinism. And he can see that the staff and congregational leadership know about the dangers of type norming and lead them in the commitment to avoid it.

An aware senior clergyperson can also work toward an environment in which conflict is accepted and valued. Too often the only conflict-resolution mechanism in the congregation is the charm of the senior clergy, and she finds herself running from one unhappy person to the next, trying to placate them. How much better, how much less co-dependent, to give examples of productive conflict, to expect people to deal with their own conflict directly, to openly recognize differences, and to cherish the different perspectives that are represented in conflict. Admittedly this is usually easier for Thinking types than for Feeling types. I was startled one day when someone said to me, "If you and I agreed on everything, then there wouldn't need to be but one of us, would there?"

It seems that the values of the MBTI have several moral claims to make on the church. First, everyone should be included. "No Outcasts" is a valid principle, provided it is understood (at least) in these terms. There must be a place for those with S and J preferences. "A place" means a theological articulation consistent with their values, some power to influence the outcome of decisions, and some reflection of their values in such areas as liturgical planning.

Second, the power must be shared. It is one thing to recognize the desire for control on the part of the Js, but quite an undesirable other to reason that because they desire it they must receive it. It is one thing for the church unintentionally to set an unwelcoming environment for one group and quite another for that group to leave because they would rather be completely in control of a small, schismatic congregation than share *any* power in the original one. Besides, a group composed only of Js runs the risk of self-destructing because of the control needs of its members! We need one another, according both to the biblical doctrine of spiritual gifts and the insights of the MBTI, and we must be willing to trust and share control with one another, lest the voice of one or several types be silenced.

There are theological consequences to these reflections. Can a congregation in a "liberal" denomination put forth with integrity, for example, a "conservative" reading of Scripture alongside the present reading? Consider, for instance, any of the stories of Jesus against the Pharisees—is that a clear case of iNtuitive against Sensing type? If it is, it is *not* the Good News for the Sensing types! Can we affirm what in the Jewish tradition Jesus affirmed, along with prophetically denying what he denied? Can we proclaim a "wisdom" Gospel as well as a "prophetic" Gospel and not have two different Gospels (Brueggeman 1978)?

And can we hold up with integrity the SJ as a model of Christian life alongside *all* the other temperaments? Many is the sermon I have heard (and, unfortunately, preached) that urged the listeners to become more open to trying new things, more spontaneous and trusting, more open to seeing the true reality behind the world of perceived objects—which is easy to hear as, "Change your type (S) to mine (N) and be saved!" In terms of the type-sensitivity that I am suggesting, this is truly demonic preaching!

Is One Type More Christian Than Another?

John Sanford, in his book *The Kingdom Within*, examines the Gospel passages in which the typological characteristics of Jesus are described. He concludes that Jesus was well-developed in all four functions as well as in his masculine and feminine sides, and that he had a strong ego. "It is apparent," concludes Sanford, "that we have here in Jesus of Nazareth the paradigm of the whole man, the prototype of all human development, a truly individual person, and therefore someone unique" (Sanford 1970, p. 35). Sanford's work is on psychological wholeness according to Jung's description, but his noting the strength and balance of Jesus' four functions is to the point: Jesus does not provide a type-preferential model for Christians.

Other writers seem to differ. For example, Oswald and Kroeger say that INFP is a "holy person" type, and that Jesus was probably an INFP or INFJ (Oswald 1988, p 52). As an INFP myself, I am pleased at being thought to have a head start toward holiness, but my knowledge of type leads me to disagree with them. I believe that they stereotype the types as Jung did, describing the pure types and not taking into account the auxiliary function. They further caricature holiness (and INFxs) by identifying holiness with a particular type. Finally, they use their type-assignments to prescribe job descriptions within the church far too rigidly.

The congregation is a holy people. The collective noun "people" is popularly misunderstood in this individualistic age, but it is necessary to understand the holiness of the congregation. Holiness is inclusive. Paul did not write about spiritual gifts without grounding his ideas in the body of Christ (Edwards 1988), and Paul's conviction is that all the various individual gifts find their rightful place in the organic whole. He urges his readers not to waste their time desiring the more popular gifts, gifts that they don't have, but to use the gifts they have with humility and assertiveness. He might have said that, taken all together, the congregation makes one whole person.

The same argument holds for psychological types, which are other ways of describing gifts (Harbaugh 1988). All are needed, each has a necessary function, and discipline is required to hear, value, and honor the contributions of each type. No one type is more Christian than another; what is Christian is a congregation using all its gifts harmoniously in working for God's justice (shalem) in the world.

CHAPTER III

Myers, Briggs, and Jung Meet Will Schutz at the Board Meeting

It is Thursday evening, and the meeting time of the Board of Elders of the congregation is drawing near. All across town, board members are preparing for the meeting.

Neal Thomason is preparing to attend because the committee that he chairs, the Long-Range Planning Committee, is making a presentation at the meeting. The committee has worked for most of a year to write a five-year plan for the congregation, and tonight is the final vote. Neal's mind is on his presentation and the vote that the elders will take afterward. He knows the plan is a good one, logical and well thought-out, and he believes that if he can make the elders see the logic of it, they will certainly vote for it. He is working on his talk, thinking especially about how to persuade the fuzzies of the value of the plan. "Fuzzies" is a nickname that Neal and a good friend of his use as a kind of shorthand for a small group of the Board of Elders. They are the ones who take up time at the meeting with personal issues, who often oppose good, tightly-argued proposals because their feelings are involved. Neal believes that they are a drag on progress, and he wants to be prepared for them, so that they will not sabotage a perfectly good, logical plan.

Nora Franklin is probably one of the fuzzies that Neal is thinking about. As she prepares for the meeting, she is thinking about her friend Martha Goodwin whom she will pick up for the ride to the meeting. They alternate picking each other up for the meeting, and this is Nora's month to drive.

If Martha were not on the Board at the same time as Nora, the meeting would be a lot less attractive to Nora; in fact, she's pretty sure she would not have let her name be put up for election. It just felt better to have someone at the meeting that you knew understood how you felt about the things the Board voted on and who would support you no matter what.

Nora thought about her attempts to make the Board a friendlier place. She had proposed that the first part of each meeting be devoted to a sharing session, "Just a few minutes," she said, "to catch up with each other. After all, we don't see each other except in church, and we're so much on the run then that we don't have time to talk. How can a group of people make good decisions when they don't know each other?" Her proposal was accepted by a close vote of the Board, but when the meetings began there were only a few people there. Most of the members missed the sharing session; they came in time for the business part of the meeting, "the real meeting," as one of them put it. After one more meeting, at which Nora and Martha were the only ones who showed up for the sharing session, the meetings went back to their previous, Robert's-Rules-of-Order pattern: opening prayer, minutes of the previous meeting, finance report, old business, new business. Nora sighed. The other people on the board were such good people, but they seemed to want to spend as little time in each others' company as possible. "How much they are missing!" thought Nora with a little sadness.

Sam Jennings did not think that he was missing much. He had contributed a great deal of money to the church and a great deal of time to making it function as a smooth-running organization. He was looking forward to a well-run meeting in which decisions would be made in an orderly way. Sam liked the minister, who, according to church law, presided at the Board meetings. Their previous minister had run sloppy meetings that dragged on forever, sometimes until ten at night, but the present minister ran a crisp, business-like meeting. Sam usually felt good as they cranked purposefully through a heavy agenda; he liked to make decisions and put ambiguity behind him so that the congregation could run smoothly. If they could only cut out the pointless chatter of a few of the members! It just took up time and didn't contribute to the purpose of the meeting. But Sam was a kind man and would not suggest silencing them in an embarrassing way; it would reflect poorly on the organization.

Sara Peacock wasn't thinking much about the meeting, though she was a member of the Board. There had been a crisis at work, and she was home for a quick bite and a hasty hello to her family before she headed back to her office for what would probably be a late evening.

Sara liked crises. She did so well in managing them that her husband had once jokingly claimed that she manufactured crises *in order* to manage them. She had to admit that there was a little truth in his remark. She seemed to lose interest in things unless there was, as she put it, "something going on." She had missed several Board meetings due to crises at her work, and she had missed several more when the Board was running smoothly. But, as she said, anyone can handle things when there's no challenge; why should she waste her time in routine, boring meetings?

Other members of the Board made their way to the church for the seven-thirty meeting. Sam arrived first and went over the agenda once more. He estimated that they would be through by eight forty-five. As the other members arrived, they greeted each other, helped themselves to decaffeinated coffee and tea, and settled around the conference table that dominated the room.

While the minister was leading the opening prayer, Nora Franklin felt miserable. She felt so left out of this Board, that she didn't have anything to offer that they wanted, and so she resolved to say as little as possible during the meeting. That was her usual style in formal meetings.

As the minutes of the previous meeting were being read, Sam looked around the table to see who else was there. He was pleased to see Neal Thomason. Of course Neal was there to present the committee report, but Sam saw him as someone who might provide more visible leadership in the congregation, who perhaps might even chair the Board in time. Of course, Neal had some wild ideas, and he didn't get along with everyone, but his heart was usually in the right place. Sam felt good to be there himself; he just hoped no one messed up the smooth meeting with irrelevant suggestions.

The meeting proceeded smoothly through the prayer and the reading of the minutes. Mike Rausch, the Treasurer, began to present the finance report when he was interrupted by Kevin Ash, the chairman of the Properties Committee, which was formerly called the Buildings and Grounds Committee. "We need to put some money aside to have the tree moved by the back door of the parsonage. I just found today that it's rotten and could fall on the parsonage and cave in the roof. It's not a question of *can* we afford it; we *have* to afford it!"

"But there's not enough money in the account for that!" retorted Treasurer Mike Rausch. "We just replaced the pew cushions, and you remember that we were hoping for a few light months before we had any more big expenses."

"We don't have to hire an expensive tree surgeon. We could get out there and do it ourselves." This from a younger member of the Board.

"Yeah, and there goes the parsonage roof and probably our liability insurance too."

The debate continued for fifteen minutes—far too long, according to Sam Jennings, who hated the chaos that seemed to be present in the meeting. Far too long, silently agreed Nora Franklin, who abhorred the conflict and the bad feelings she knew would follow. Far too long, silently agreed Neal Thomason, who was chafing to get his report presented, the vote taken, and himself returned home for a late bowl of frozen yogurt with his wife Annie.

What is going on in the Board meeting? How can we understand the dynamics of the meeting in a way that can improve them? Could the meeting be structured to better meet some of the emotional needs of its members?

Yes to both questions, according to a theory proposed by Will Schutz (1966). Popularly dubbed the "ICA theory," Schutz's theory helps explain the dynamics of people coming into groups. The group in question could be an ongoing group or a single meeting of an ongoing group, such as the Board meeting described above. The same dynamics apply.

Schutz's theory applies to all types of people, but the different MBTI types encounter and experience the predictions of the theory in significantly different ways. After we look at the basic themes of ICA, we will look at the variations on those themes played by the MBTI types and then will look particularly at implications for newcomers.

According to Schutz's theory, when a person enters a group of people, the person will be asking certain kinds of questions, all having to do with a basic interpersonal need: being included in a group. Here are some typical questions (see Schutz 1966 and 1968); their formulation is from Turner (1977).

Inclusion Questions

–Who else is here?
–How can I be in relation to them?
–What will it cost to join this group?
–How much am I willing to pay to become a member?
–Can I trust my real self to them?
–Will they support me if the going gets tough?
–How can I get acquainted with them?

If these questions are resolved satisfactorily, the person can move on to a second set of questions, all related to the interpersonal need to be in control.

Control Questions

–Who is calling the shots here?
–How much can I push for what I want?
–Will I have to be direct or indirect to influence others?
–What do others require of me?
–Can I say what I really think and feel?
–Can I take it if they say what they really think?

And when these have been resolved to the person's satisfaction, another set can be considered, all related to the interpersonal need to express and receive expressions of affect.

Affect Questions

–Am I willing to care?
–Can I show my caring?
–What will happen if I show I care for one person before I show caring for others?
–What if no one cares for me?
–What if they do show caring for me?
–What if I don't really ever care for someone in the group?
–Will the group be able to bear it?
–Is showing affection acceptable in this group? How do I know this?

One of the implications of the ICA theory is that the issues are sequenced, that is, some kind of satisfactory resolution of the inclusion issue has to be made before control issues can even be considered, and similarly with control and affect. This makes sense. If I feel so "un-included" in the group that I don't want to have anything to do with it, I don't care who's in control and feel little desire to exert any control. And if the group is not a safe one, with someone in control and myself protected, I will not risk an overt show of affect.

Another part of ICA theory is that, when a group dissolves, the same issues are resolved in reverse order, first A, then C, and then I. For example, as a weekend group winds to a close, it is noticeable that the display of strong affect will usually cease; people will let go of the things they were responsible for; and finally there will often be some kind of ritual of ending inclusion, such as a group hug.

I realize that inclusion is very important to me, an insight that was underscored by a comment from a reader of this manuscript. He said that the thesis of the book did not move him very much, that congregations had to make decisions and move on. For him, control is more important; for me, inclusion is, otherwise I would not have gone to the trouble of writing a whole book about it. Here's to both of us—AND to those who see affect as the most important!

What went wrong with the Board of Elders' meeting? Nora Franklin was on the right track. People needed to have a time and place to deal with their inclusion issues before they could deal with control issues. What she did not realize is that people deal with those in quite different ways from the way she deals with them. Sharing sessions are not for everyone, but the inclusion level was low because little attention was paid to these issues. When it came time for the finance report, people were trying to get themselves included in the only way they had available—by arguing. Control was never an issue for the Board; they never got that far! And affect—well, who would ever think it desirable to express strong feelings at a Board meeting?

People feel included for different reasons, and the reasons depend, among other things, on their MBTI type. Some, like Neal Thomason (NT), feel included when there are people who support their ideas and projects. Others, like Sam Jennings (SJ), feel included when others support their values, especially about the institution. Still others, like Sara Peacock (SP), feel included only when their particular skills at crisis management are needed; to put it another way, their inclusion needs are low to none. Nora Franklin (NF) knows that she is included when she is personally valued by members of the group. She knows that she is personally valued when she can relate to others at a feeling level. Sharing is a way to do that.

Similarly, inclusion is approached differently by Introverts and Extraverts. Extraverts are usually willing to exert more effort to be included in a group than Introverts; they need other people, for they receive energy from them. Introverts seemingly have lower needs for inclusion than do Extraverts, but it could be that they work less hard to get their needs for inclusion met. Either way, Introverts are likely to feel less included than Extroverts. Most Introverts are used to it, take it for granted, and don't see it as a problem.

How about issues of control? Clearly, Introverts and Extraverts have different *arenas* of control, namely the inner and outer worlds. In a meeting such as the one we visited, the Introverts have little need to be in control; their desire is more generally that *someone* be in control so that they will be safe from attack in the outer world, for that is where they feel vulnerable. Introverts may feel caught in a bind. They do not see themselves as wanting to be in control, but they do not want to be controlled by anyone else either.

Judging and Perceptive functions are the control functions. Judging types often outnumber Perceptive types on boards and in management circles generally; they seek arenas to get these important needs met. So when the conflict over the tree broke out in the Board meeting (inclusion masquerading as control), it was probably the Extraverted Judging types who were most vocally represented. Others were quite involved in the conflict, but it was the Extraverts who acted out the feelings of the group, as they often do.

Affect issues are more difficult to see. At first sight the feeling types might be seem to express affect, emotions, more easily and readily. But Jung's theory says that we may think of these functions as tools. The more developed the function is, the better tool it is—that is, the more control the user will have over it. So, for feeling types, their feelings are useful, well-controlled tools. They are able to turn their feelings on or off in ways that may seem quite calculated to thinking types, whose feelings are less well controlled. Nonetheless, feelings are more important to feeling types, and they are likely to be the ones to give expression to their feelings with the same facility and nuance that thinking types give to their thoughts.

Persons of all types need for meetings to be planned in such a way that they have opportunity to resolve each of these issues. There are many ways to satisfy these needs. Some use a time of "checking in"—just telling a little about what is happening in each person's life. In a workshop, we often ask people to introduce themselves. Even something as simple as saying their names aloud helps people to state that they are present in the space; speaking their name aloud includes them, at least a little. Ice-breakers, artificial as they often seem, (and as despised as they are by Introverts!) are ways to help people deal with their inclusion needs. They give people information about other people so that they can answer some of the inclusion questions: Who else is here? Can I get anything from being in this group? Do I have anything to offer?

How may we use our type understanding to help with the problem of newcomers? I call it a problem because visitors seem to make decisions about joining that have little to do with the way the congregation sees itself. A congregation may have its newcomer program in place and active; they may greet visitors at the door and after worship; they may call on them during the first two days after their initial visit; they may partner them with members; they may have newcomer orientations or classes and a whole program of incorporating newcomers into the congregation—and then someone will say that they decided to go elsewhere because the minister waved his arms when he preached, or there weren't enough social justice programs, or the congregation seemed cold. Many staff people who work with newcomers have been tempted to throw up their hands in frustration. "What do they want, anyway?"

I believe that the MBTI can help us to be more effective in greeting and incorporating newcomers. We can do it by asking, as in Chapter I, "What do they need, based on their type?" We'll look at the four temperaments for simplicity.

SJs need to have a good, smooth-running institution and will exert themselves considerably to maintain one. They are attracted to the kind of power that goes with organizational rank and are lovers of order. Ambiguity is uncomfortable for them, and so they need clarity of preaching and teaching as well as clarity of organizational structure. "How is the organization structured?" they may ask. "Where are the power buttons? And how does one get anything done in this congregation?"

Many people think of the organizational structure as the skeleton of the parish, hidden from the outside by the skin and flesh. Not so SJs; to them the institution pretty much is the congregation, and they want to know who is in control and how the control is managed in the congregation. Organizational diagrams are helpful; they present power structures, at least the officially perceived ones, in visual (sensing) form. SJs want to know what the organizational roles are and how one gets to fill those roles. Institutional tradition is important; in strongly SJ congregations, photographs of past ordained ministers often line the walls of the congregational common room. Archives, plaques commemorating past gifts and achievements, traditional liturgy—all can be "flags" to SJs who are thinking about joining. As is also true with the other types, they might not be consciously looking for such things, but their keen sense of "Is this a friendly environment?" is offended if these or similar things are not present.

According to some studies, SJs are represented in greater numbers in mainline congregations than in the larger population. One reason is that most congregations are places where one can find an organizational role easily; such roles are often pressed on newcomers. Such congregations may take on even more characteristics of an institution, perhaps even to the exclusion of other ways of understanding the congregation.

For an SP the organization is still the focus of this interest, but it is the organization in crisis. SPs tend to be attracted to crises and are at their best when routine structures break down. They tend not to be found in heavily SJ congregations and in fact are underrepresented in mainline congregations.

What opportunities are there for SPs in the newcomer orientation? Is there a crisis ministry team, whose members are on call to respond to emergencies in the congregation? Is there a program in trouble, which needs good leadership to be renewed? In many congregations the congregational style works against attracting SPs. Great importance is put on maintaining a smoothly running organization, which satisfies the SJs but will bore the SPs. Care must be taken to involve the SP in important areas of organizational repair.

Where the SJ and SP interests are largely organizational, the NT and NFs see the congregation in a different light. To them the organization itself is less important than the people in it. For NFs the congregation is a place for people and possibilities. They need to hear stories of personal ministries in which persons are helped and lives are changed. "If this congregation can accept and help those people, then there is a place here for me." A congregation rich in small groups will be especially attractive to many INFs, for small groups provide a place to relate to a few people at the feeling level. The warmth of the clergy and staff will be particularly important to NFs, and the warmth of the congregation may well determine whether they stay or seek their church home elsewhere. For them, task- or achievement-oriented ministry is less important than people-oriented ministry. Also, the classical spiritual life is more attractive to NFs than to any other type. Prayer, journaling, prayer and Bible-study groups, may all be attractive and inviting to them. NFs may not fit any of the classic patterns of spirituality, especially if they're Extraverted, but they desire support in their spiritual life and will gladly respond when it is offered.

The NT is the possibility-oriented thinker. Where an NF considering joining a congregation will be looking for people to relate to, an NT will be looking for people to join her in a just cause. Peace and justice ministries, ecology and nature ministries, economic justice ministries—all may be attractive to the NT newcomer. The justice positions of the denomination may attract or repel the NT newcomer. The congregation is a place to get something done that is directly values-related; people are important for what they can bring to the project, not primarily for their relationships.

Good theology is especially important to thinking types. NTs can take in highly symbolic theology, but it must be rational; it is possible to hurt a thinking type's thinkings, just as it is possible to hurt a feeling person's feelings.

How to cover all these bases in a newcomer orientation? First, conduct a parish survey of the programs, sorted by which program would attract (at least) the four temperaments. Be rigorous; your congregation might be lacking in programs appealing to one or more temperaments. Then recruit a person of the appropriate type to present to newcomers the programs that should appeal to that type. They speak the language, and they should be enthusiastic about "their" programs. Give them equal time. Let *them* decide on the medium for their message. They may be able to tailor the medium to the temperament in a most creative way. When they speak, listen for characteristic language of the type. If you summarize, use their language.

And design the newcomer orientation for at least the four temperaments. Make it well organized and fast-moving enough for the SJs and personal enough for the NFs; emphasize projects and opportunities enough for the NTs, and make it urgent-sounding enough to interest the SPs.

So much for the newcomer orientation. Now let's look at some key indicators of the congregation's style.

Look at the bulletin boards and the brochures that present the program or ministries of the congregation. Do they tell something about the organization structure, with committees and titles (SJ)? Do they tell something about how to get organizationally involved (SJ)? Do they have pictures of people having a good time with each other (NF)? Do they describe ministries in organizational terms only (committee, task force), in needs-of-people terms only (AIDS care team, hospital visitors), or both? Are there logos and symbols (N) as well as clear instructions (S)? Are there indicators of goals achieved (NT) as well as organizations maintained (SJ)? Is there the implication that there is never a crisis, never a ripple in the organizational flow? What is appealing to some—a smoothly running organization—will discourage others. Are all the temperaments represented roughly equally? Are they represented in their own language?

Look at the sign in front of the church. Does it tell just the congregation's name or does it have at least one person's name as well? Does it give the newcomer enough information to engage the congregation at an initial level (phone number, service times, office location)? Does it give the person's title as well as the name?

Look at the cards in the pews, the ones that people put in the offering plate to let the leaders know of their needs. Is the language institutional—committees, joining, receiving sacraments—or personal needs—sickness, new births—or both?

Pay attention to the announcements in church. Are they about people or organizations? Both are important.

Pay attention to the sermons. Are they mostly thinking sermons, feeling sermons, or is there a mixture of both? Are they exhortations to inner personal transformation or more dutiful service? Both are needed. Do they have a lot of concrete detail, like birds and flowers and children, or are they more symbolic and poetic? Both are needed. Do they exhort people to get organized, to make a decision (today, for Christ), or to stay loose and flexible about life (one day at a time)? Both are needed.

Look at the direction signs. Are they clear, so that newcomers can easily find their way around, even on a busy Sunday morning? Is the Sunday schedule posted visibly, perhaps in a number of places? Or do people have to know where their classroom is from long experience? ("If you have to ask, you must be new.") These are Sensing needs, but they help iNtuitives also.

Look at the process for joining the congregation. Is it a clear, step-by-step process, or are there places that are fuzzy? Is there someone to follow up with newcomers to help them through the steps? Is sufficient attention paid to their inclusion and control needs, as influenced by their type?

Finally, look at the leadership training process in the congregation, by whatever name it is called. Does the leadership understand type differences, and are the people in leadership positions sympathetic with the idea that different types have different legitimate needs, or are they still wedded to the notion that everyone is really alike and should be like themselves? A module in the Board orientation on type differences and how they impact the congregation is a must.

It is not difficult to make a congregational environment—the buildings, signs, printed matter, etc.—more all-type-friendly. An eye aware of the needs of the various types and some imagination is all that's needed. We turn now to something more complex, the spirituality of the congregation as it is influenced by type.

CHAPTER IV

Congregational Spirituality

The idea that different people respond differently to the experience of transcendence is not new. Huston Smith, in his book *The Religions of Man* (1958), identifies four yogas of the ancient Hindu religion that correspond in some measure to Jung's four functions.

The first yoga is the way to God through knowledge, called jnana yoga. In this yoga, one becomes aware through hearing that the infinite fount of being lies at the center of one's own being and, through thinking, lets the reality of that fount of being take on life. For example, one may examine one's own use of language, reflecting on one's use of the word "my." Or one may through thinking shift one's identification from the passing to the eternal part of one's own being, for example by thinking of oneself in the third person. This is clearly a thinking person's approach to the mystery.

The second yoga is the way to God through love, called bhakti yoga. In this yoga, one finds the geyser of love that lies in the heart and directs it toward God. One adores God with all one's feeling soul. This yoga uses symbols, rituals, myths, multiple images of God, devotion to God in the form of one's chosen ideal—anything that will connect one with God through feeling and imagination. The yogin grows in the relationship with God: from a dependent relationship (such as servant-master, receiver-giver, or protected-protector), through friendship, then parental (in which the devotee looks on God as if God were his child) finally moving into the relationship of lover to beloved. This yoga touches the affect and imagination and would likely be suitable for NF types.

The third yoga Smith calls the way to God through work, or karma yoga. Here one throws oneself into work with all one's might, designating the work as one's pathway to God. Every action, every moment is communion with God. The work of Brother Lawrence and his practice of the presence of God comes to mind here and the idea of work as sacramental.

One may practice karma yoga with either a bhakti or a jnana flavor. In the former one does the work for God's sake, putting all of one's feelings and energy into it, and practices becoming detached from the outcome of the work. In the latter, one practices detachment from the empirical self and identifies instead with the eternal Self that stands separate from it.

The fourth yoga is the way to God through psychological exercise, called raja yoga. This way is understood as a series of experiments on one's spirit. The purpose is to test the Hindu view of man as four layers: body, conscious personality, individual subconscious, and Being itself. The method is a way of discipline, taking on five abstentions, five observances, control of the body and of the breath, closing the windows of the senses, calming the mind through meditation, and finally union with God.

These descriptions are in no sense complete and are meant only to suggest the differences in flavor between the four yogas.

It is interesting to speculate about the extent to which Jung's early familiarity with Hinduism, learned through his mother, (see Jung 1963) influenced his theory of psychological types. There are striking similarities between the functions and the yogas.

Similar ideas are not difficult to find in the Christian tradition. Tilden Edwards, in his book *Spiritual Friend* (1980), describes four paths of spirituality. These are not limited to the Christian tradition, but include it.

The first is the path of devotion, in which one cultivates a personal, intimate sense of God, using much the same images as bhakti yoga. The intuitions and feelings are used in prayers of petition, praise, and thanksgiving. The beauty of nature may be emphasized or charismatic gifts such as tongue-speaking, prophecy, and healing.

The second path is the path of action, which focuses on moral concerns, the good, the righteous. The image of God in this path is the redeeming judge, calling us to righteousness and justice, to personal correction. In this path we are to fight corruption and apathy and defend the oppressed and powerless through moral teaching and disciplined action.

This path is a Sensing-Thinking person's path, emphasizing justice, fairness, and action.

Edwards' third path is the path of knowledge, subdivided into analytical and intuitive paths. In the analytical path, one is given over to reason. It is a way of understanding based on logical considerations. One seeks precise, cognitive symbols of the Holy in relation to human life and attempts to live a life out of those symbols, correcting them through reflection on lived experience.

In the path of intuitive knowledge, one follows a subtle and direct apprehension of the truth, unmediated through symbols or other intellects. This is the path of Zen koans, parables, paradoxes, and psychic powers.

Edwards lists a fourth path, called "fighting it all the way," which many will recognize as their own. It is the path of iconoclasm, idol-smashing. At its best it is the spirit of Protestantism, testing every symbol, every expression of God's presence and activity against one's own logic. At its worst it becomes sour and defensive, often leading to despair.

One use of these types in spirituality is to help our awareness of balance. Each of the types is good and valid but on occasion may become stale or unfruitful. During those times, experienced spiritual directors may suggest a discipline of the opposite type, using a less well-developed function. An experienced monastic spiritual director has told me that he often puts Ns to work in the garden of the monastery; the experience uses their Sensing to literally "ground" them. Simone Weil's internal sense of call sent her to work in a factory, countering her NT temperament with SJ work.

At the same time, it must be remembered that the MBTI has to do with psychological type and is not properly a description of types of spirituality. It may be desirable to "balance" the functions or to develop the inferior function through confronting the shadow, but it is possible in this way to stray far from any central tradition of Christian spirituality, which generally has to do with loving awareness and compassionate action in the name of Christ. The purposes of Jungian individuation and Christian conversion have some overlap, but they are far from identical.

This distinction and these schemes of type and spirituality lead us into a recurring and vexed question: What is the relation between spirituality and psychology?

Many people identify the two. Jung, for example, averred to the end that he was not writing theology but empirical science, i.e. psychology, yet many assume that because he speaks of God and Christ he was really writing spirituality, and his language and ideas have been widely used in spirituality. (See for example many of Morton Kelsey's books, including Kelsey 1976, 1972, and 1983).

Others argue along another line. We are one, they say—body, soul, and spirit. Therefore any division, for example that between psychology and spirituality, is artificial. Spirituality and psychology are really one because we are one.

Many writers have attempted to synthesize the two, or at least to blur the differences, along these or some other lines.

A more naive version is found in the loose usage of the term "psychology" in our culture to mean anything that happens inside us that is not physical. This is congruent with the medical-psychiatric practice of labeling a condition "psychosomatic" or "psychogenic" when all known organic causes have been ruled out; "psycho" here means "non-physical," a decidedly materialist definition. To accept the definition is to accept the assumption underlying the definition. There is a great deal more to the interior life than psychology can or desires to understand.

I propose to maintain a distinction between the two. By psychology I understand the discipline that is practiced in university psychology departments, a social science based on hypothesis and experiment which leads to theories and then to new hypotheses. By spirituality I understand the various ideas, practices, and experiences by which people understand and practice their relationship with the mystery of God. One can attempt a psychology of spirituality, and one could attempt a spirituality of psychology—Gerald May has written a psychology that arises from the experience of contemplation (1982)—but psychology and spirituality are different.

My reason for maintaining the distinction was well stated by May when he wrote of the tendency of psychology to overwhelm spirituality in most attempts to synthesize the two. May is particularly helpful with his distinction between "willful" and "willing." Willfulness is based on my desire to be in control. I desire a certain outcome and act intentionally so as to achieve it. If I achieve the outcome that I desire, then my action was effective; otherwise it is not. Science, including psychology, tends to be willful.

Thomas Moore has made the same distinction between spirituality and psychology in his recent book *Care of the Soul* (Moore 1992). He would merge the two but that would mean "the end of psychology as we have known it altogether because it is essentially modern, secular, and ego-centered" (p. xv). He, too, is trying to articulate an interiority that is not psychological in order to care for the soul, and he goes to pre-modern writers to support his ideas. I believe that psychology has a useful place in soul-making, but that something other than psychology, something at the same time much older, much newer, and much wiser, must lie at the heart of the spiritual journey.

Willingness is a different mode of consciousness than willfulness. It is more open, more receptive, not tied to the outcome of actions. It is related to the willful mode in somewhat the same way that the right brain is to the left (understanding these symbolically and not physiologically). Spirituality as I understand it has to do with the movement between willfulness and willingness.

In our culture it seems to be a cultural value that willfulness overwhelms willingness. That, I believe, is one reason for the institution of the Sabbath day—to set aside and protect a time to enter into the mode of willingness—and it is why the Sabbath is less and less observed.

Science is a child of the Enlightenment, and its purpose is to explain observable phenomena in terms of other observable phenomena, with the fewest possible additional concepts. There is no room there for explanations of natural phenomena in terms of God's action or purpose. As a science, psychology has no room for transcendence, for mystery. It need not, should not, in order to be true to its Enlightenment origins, but it hews to those origins at the cost of restricting its purview to a rather narrow range of phenomena. It will always miss what Lonergan (1970) calls the empirical residue, the part that is left after the scientific explanation is given. Scientific understandings are inevitably anti-mysterious, always reductionistic. The empirical residue is vast compared with the phenomena that can, even in principle, be accounted for by scientific means. Therefore neither psychology nor any other modern science can ever be an adequate method or provide an adequate language for spiritual phenomena. Typology is quite inadequate to describe the richness and nuance of spiritual experience. Especially to be avoided are tables or charts that claim to correlate type with typical experience, belief, or practice—another Procrustean bed that psychology offers to spirituality!

Having made those claims, how may the MBTI types be used with authenticity in spirituality, particularly in congregational spirituality?

One way is to help people differentiate from each other. It is true that there is, as Buddhist teacher Alan Watts claims, a taboo against knowing who you are. The type indicator can provide a first step in knowing that you are not "everyone." Many people will assent to the statement that "God loves everyone" without having an intuitive or felt knowledge that God loves them, in all their particularity. They tend to believe that all spiritual disciplines are equally valid for themselves and tend to see their own point of view, their own feelings and perceptions and judgments, as a norm. The MBTI can help them to come to the first awareness that they are not identical to everyone else, that different valid perceptions are possible, and that perhaps God loves them in a particular way, different from the way God loves others, which suits them more. That self-differentiation is an important part of the faith journey.

Another way of using typology in spiritual work is given in Michael and Norrisey's *Prayer and Temperament* (1984). By analyzing many accounts of spiritual life, they observe that there are four main styles of spirituality. They label them with names of saints of the church. In each case, we respond to the mystery in part according to our type, but our response is also open and not finally determined by our type. At our best, we respond willingly, but the shape of our willingness is influenced by our type. Thus the typology may be useful for suggesting approaches to prayer or for legitimizing certain styles of prayer as "really prayer," but a good spiritual director will be sensitive to God's call and the person's desire for God that doesn't fit with their or any other type. In this respect, our type is something like our physiology: it may pose some limitations and opportunities because of its specificity, but does not finally determine God's call or our response.

In Michael and Norrisey's book there are four main styles of spirituality, labeled by temperament. The NF style is called Augustinian prayer. It is imaginative and involves a personal relationship with God. Augustinians need a lot of feeding, like a plant, through books and retreats. They find God in the future and are often "in the future," imagining what the Kingdom will be like.

The SJ style is called Ignatian prayer after the founder of the Society of Jesuits, Ignatius Loyola. (An N question: Is it more than coincidence that the initials of the Sensing-Judging temperament are the same as those of Loyola's order?) They value discipline, order, continuity with the past.

The NT style is called Thomistic prayer after St. Thomas Aquinas and is characterized by an orderly progression of thought from cause to effect. To other types, NT prayer may seem more like study and reflection than like prayer; I have found NTs to be surprised and pleased when their prayer of this type is labeled such.

Finally, the SP style is named after St. Francis of Assisi. It is open, free-flowing, spontaneous, informal. It appeals to the five senses, and people in this style often pray using music, dance, or a paint brush.

Michael and Norrisey point out that the Benedictine way of prayer seems to combine all four functions; thus it may be seen as the most inclusive of the styles. It is described formally in four stages, although in practice the stages are not usually clear-cut. *Lectio divina,* the slow, meditative reading of sacred texts, uses the senses to get the facts of the text. It lets the facts sink in, broods over them, allows them to enter the imagination and the memory. *Meditatio* uses Thinking and iNtuiting to bring to mind memories, associations, and hunches related to the text. There is always room here for inspiration, for something "out of the blue." The third step, *oratio*, uses Feeling to respond to the passage and to the iNtuitions from the previous stages. In this stage one responds, either silently or aloud, through thoughts, words, desires, feelings, resolutions, decisions, commitments, dedications, sorrow, or gratitude. Finally, in *contemplatio*, the fourth step, one simply sits and enjoys the presence of God.

Note that meditatio and contemplatio, as used here, have roughly opposite meanings from meditation and contemplation as they are commonly used today.

In congregational spirituality, as in the other chapters, the question is "What do they need?" Here I will make some suggestions about the needs of the different temperaments and functions in the area of spirituality.

First, the congregation needs diverse opportunities for spiritual expression and experience. The opportunities should be provided intentionally, not left to chance, and by and large they should be provided by persons of that type. Some NFs, for example, need to take the lead in providing opportunity for other NFs to find what they need in the congregation.

This may seem to go against the denominational tradition of worship, but it need not. The standard Sunday worship needs to touch enough bases typologically to keep everyone fed, but it does not need to be everyone's main meal. It will typically be balanced among the types, as Benedictine spirituality tends to be. From a typological point of view, it is no accident that Benedictine worship was the backbone for a central tradition of Christian worship for centuries. It provides for a "catholicity of type." For example, the SJs will get many of their needs met through well-ordered, traditional worship in which they know what will happen and therefore can participate easily. The NFs will need more opportunities for intimacy and imagination, opportunities that are not found in most congregational worship services. But many congregations have small groups; why not make them an intentional part of the congregation if they are not, and have some worship opportunities that are more suitable to NFs—more opportunity for imagination and to express their feelings in worship? In some congregations that might mean a monthly prayer-and-praise service; in others, a contemplative communion service with simple symbols—a Bible, a candle, a plant—and much silence (attractive to the Introverted NFs); in still others, movement and singing as part of the informal liturgy.

Occasional opportunities for spiritual growth may be considered along the same lines—building intentionally on what is already present. For example, retreats are important occasions for spiritual growth, especially for INFs. Building a balanced retreat program between silent times and times of fellowship may attract ENFs, as will a warm, personal retreat leader. Are you likely to draw many SPs to such a retreat? No, but their spiritual needs may be met in different ways—perhaps through service on the congregation's crisis ministry team, or through short-term hands-on opportunities for ministry, such as youth ministry, a wilderness weekend, rope-climbing team-building experiences, decorating the church for Easter or Christmas, or going to Haiti to build playgrounds. Providing congregational opportunities for each of the temperaments to find spiritual food can be an important ministry in itself.

Another important task is helping the congregation understand the rudiments of type difference. No one needs to become an expert on type, but enough needs to be said to help people realize that there are other people in the congregation with different needs than theirs. It is a salutary confrontation, and type is a gentle, well-researched way to present it.

Here is a simple-minded way to think through some of the implications of type in your present congregational structure. On four sheets of paper, list all the sub-organizations and para-organizations of the congregation. By para-organization I mean organizations that are not part of the congregation but which affect some members. Cursillo, for example, may be one such organization; the judicatory is another. Use the four temperaments, NF, SP, NT, and SJ, as headings for the four sheets, and list the organizations under the temperament they mostly attract. Some —a few—might be listed more than once. Generally the organizations will have pretty clear primary functions: the SJ organizations will keep the institution instituting; the NF organizations will meet for personal/spiritual growth; the NT organizations will meet for some aspect of achievement and excellence; and the SP organizations will meet to meet crises, negotiate risks, and do hands-on ministry where little structure is present. Are most of the organizations SJ ones? If so, where do the NFs go for growth? Is there anything for SPs, or is the congregation so domi-nantly SJ that there is "never" an opportunity for a crisis? Is there a place for NT clarity and project-oriented achievement in the congregation?

And are these efforts recognized and encouraged as legitimate spirituality? Any activity that I do which has as its intent to relate myself to God is a spiritual activity. There is no one way, no right way. God seems to honor our desire and respond to us in whatever way we seek. There are many spiritual activities that have not traditionally been seen as prayer, such as service to the needy or theological reflection. They are legitimate spiritual activities if they are done with that intent, and the congregation should affirm them as such.

For those who have no idea where to begin in the spiritual life, a seminar in spiritual gifts may be appropriate. This affirms each person's uniqueness, while also giving some idea of how to work with people who are different. This is especially important for high-school youth, who are naturally working to find their uniqueness and giftedness. One way to approach spiritual gifts is via the MBTI, taking each of the types as a particular gift and asking how it fits with the others to make a whole body (see Harbaugh 1988). St. Paul's notion of the body as being composed of many harmoniously functioning members is important here, because people work together best when each person is working in his or her own type.

Working toward a type-inclusive congregation has its costs, but the benefits may be seen in livelier worship, greater participation in committees and meetings, better decisions, and deeper commitment to projects of service and human need. If type-related needs are well and intentionally met, each member of the congregation will have a greater sense of belonging, of feeling included and valued, and of contributing to something larger than he or she could achieve alone.

APPENDIX

A Congregation Checklist

This checklist is not meant to be comprehensive, but rather to stimulate your imagination as you think about your congregational life.

Teaching and Learning

Opportunity for talking about the material with others (E)

Opportunity for thinking alone and writing about the material (I)

Opportunity for immediate response to the material and time to talk it through (E)

Opportunity and time to think it through before responding (I)

Learning by doing, tasting, touching, sensing, seeing the practicality of the material (S, expecially ES)

Learning by taking it one step at a time, building the big picture up from the details (S)

Learning by seeing possibilities, designing a better way (N)

Learning by seeing the big picture, then working down to the details (N)

Learning by reflecting on how the material fits with my values, how it affects people (F)

Learning by understanding how the material hangs together logically, by analyzing (T)

Learning in a more structured environment (J)

Learning in a more spontaneous environment (P)

Management and meetings

Let's have a tight agenda and brief, decision-oriented, efficient meetings (SJ)

Let's have an open agenda, taking time to relate at a feeling level and time to include people's concerns (NF)

Let's just deal with the urgent stuff, leave the routine stuff for someone else (SP)

What is supposed to be the output from this black box called a congregation? Let's work on clarifying that and streamlining everything that doesn't directly contribute (NT)

Crisis ministry, crisis task force (SP)

Committees chosen typologically appropriate to their purpose, with the type differences regarded as gifts to the committee's work

Conflict accepted, valued, openly addressed, and worked through

For everyone: some time for inclusion, resolving the inclusion issues in their own style

Worship, including preaching

Clear, rational objective sermons—"preach on justice and fairness issues, help me to understand and act (T)—and keep it brief!"

Sermons on personal values—personal examples—"let the preacher show she or he cares about what they are preaching about—preach on harmony among people" (F)

Orderly, traditional worship (SJ)

Inspiring, moving worship (NF)

Stick to the tried and true patterns (J)

Try something new (P)

What's so bad about the elder brother of the prodigal son? (SJ)

What's so bad about the prodigal son? (P)

Powerful symbols that operate at a deep, connective level (N)

Encouragement to duty, responsibility (SJ)

Staff

Staff of a variety of types, free to express their typological style openly and visibly, with support from other staff members

Awareness of type differences, sensitivity to type issues, and some facility at using the language of the complementary type

Publications, Signs, and Bulletin Boards

Monitored for type chauvinism—a balance, attractive to all types

Organization on display for the SJs—committees, meetings, minutes, chairs, and other roles

People on display for the Fs—pictures, names of people, some expression of feeling as well as fact

Possibilities on display for the Ns—opportunities, suggestions, invitations

"Where are the openings for me to get in, or are all the pieces finished perfectly? I need some imperfections! Where are the experiential opportunities for me?" for the Ps

"Everything in control? Good," say the Js.

Pictures of people having a good time with each other (NF)

Ministries described in organizational terms (SJ) as well as achievement terms (NT) as well as personal-needs-met terms (NF) as well as crises-met-and-managed terms (SP)

* * * * *

Using the MBTI Without an "Expert"

"I don't have anyone with the credentials to order, administer, and interpret the MBTI, yet I'd like to use it with (a group in) my congregation."

There are several ways to help people identify their type without using the MBTI questionnaire. They are less accurate, but quite adequate for teaching about MBTI and for the kinds of uses suggested in this book.

The first is an exercise from Lawrence, "Thinking About Mental Habits" (1982, 2). It is a series of forced-choice descriptions, describing each extreme of one of the four MBTI axes. For example, the E-I axis is described by the statements "likes action and variety" (E) and "likes quiet and time to consider things" (I).

I have used this exercise with groups of adults and groups of teenagers in the following way. I ask the participants to imagine a line down the middle of the floor. One end represents one extreme, the other end the other extreme. "I'm going to read two descriptions, and I want you to place yourself at THIS end of the room (pointing) if you agree completely with the FIRST description, and at THAT end of the room (pointing) if you agree with the SECOND description. Otherwise, put yourself somewhere in between." I then read the first two descriptions and give them time to move into place. "Now look around and see where everyone is. Make a mental note of where you are. Now here's the second set of descriptions." After going through the descriptions for the E-I axis, I briefly introduce the concepts of Extraversion and Introversion and say that they have placed themselves on the E-I scale by where they stood. Then we go through the other scales similarly.

There is another way to introduce the four functions T-F and S-N, using an exercise modeled on Lawrence's "Eat-An-Apple" exercise (Lawrence 1982, p. 22). If I'm working with a church group, instead of asking them to eat an apple (itself an excellent teaching exercise), I ask them to pair off and assign a bible story, one with a vivid narrative. One pair is to read it and respond and the other is to record the responses of the first.

I ask them to mark a sheet of paper in four quadrants. Then the reader reads the story and answers questions similar to Lawrence's questions. "As you read the story, what are some of the sense impressions you notice? Just sense impressions—touch, taste, colors, smells, sounds, etc. The recorder should list all you can remember in the FIRST quadrant. List facts only."

"Now, in the SECOND quadrant, list all the memories and associations you associate with the story. What does it remind you of? List any people or situations from childhood, stories, myths, poems, fairy tales, proverbs, superstitions."

"Now, in the THIRD quadrant, list any logical conclusions you can draw about the story from what you've put in the first two quadrants—logical conclusions based on facts and intuitions."

"Now, in the FOURTH quadrant, list your feeling judgments: how you feel about doing this exercise, how you felt about the story, how you felt about the outcome of the story."

"Now I would guess that you found some of the quadrants easier to complete than others. For some you had lots of responses, and for others it was a strain to come up with one or two. Here are the letters that go with each one: S with the FIRST, N with the SECOND, T with the THIRD, and F with the FOURTH. Which ones were the easiest for you? Which ones the most difficult?"

REFERENCES

Bridges, William. *The Character of Organizations: Using Jungian Type in Organizational Development.* Palo Alto, CA: Consulting Psychologists Press, 1992.

Brueggemann, Walter. *The Prophetic Imagination.* Philadelphia: Fortress Press, 1978.

Campbell, Joseph. *The Portable Jung.* New York: Viking Press, 1971.

Edwards, Lloyd. *Discerning Your Spiritual Gifts.* Boston: Cowley Publications, 1988.

Edwards, Tilden. *Spiritual Friend: Reclaiming the Gift of Spiritual Direction.* New York: Paulist Press, 1980.

Fordham, Frieda. *An Introduction to Jung's Psychology.* Baltimore: Penguin Books, 1953.

Hall, Calvin S. and Vernon J. Nordby. *A Primer of Jungian Psychology.* New York: New American Library, 1973).

Harbaugh, Gary. *God's Gifted People.* Minneapolis: Augsburg Press, 1988.

Jung, Carl G., Tr. H. G. Baynes. *Psychological Types.* New York: Harcourt Brace, 1923. [Originally published in German as *Psychologische Typen* (Zurich: Rascher Verlag, 1921) and as Vol.

6, *Gesammelte Werke* (Zurich: Rascher Verlag, 1960). This book is Vol. 6, Part I of *The Collected Works of Carl G. Jung*, Tr. F. C. Hull, (Bollingen Series 6, Princeton, NJ: Princeton University Press, 1971).]

——*Memories, Dreams, Reflections,* Tr. Richard and Clara Winston. New York: Pantheon Press, 1963.

——*Man and His Symbols.* New York: Doubleday, 1964.

Kelsey, Morton T. *Companions on the Inner Way: The Art of Spiritual Guidance.* New York: Crossroad, 1983.

——*Encounter with God: A Theology of Christian Experience:* Minneapolis: Bethany Fellowship, 1972.

——*The Other Side of Silence: A Guide to Christian Meditation.* New York: Paulist Press, 1976.

Kiersey, David and Marilyn Bates. *Please Understand Me.* Del Mar, CA: Prometheus Nemesis Books, 1978.

Lawrence, Gordon. *People Types and Tiger Stripes: A Practical Guide to Learning Styles.* 2d ed. Gainesville, FL: Center for Application of Psychological Type, 1982.

——ed. *Home Study Guide for the MBTI Training Program.* Gainesville, FL: Center for Application of Psychological Type, 1988.

Lonergan, Bernard J. G. *Insight: A Study of Human Understanding.* 3rd ed. New York: Philosophical Library, 1970.

May, Gerald G., M.D. *Will & Spirit: A Contemplative Psychology.* San Francisco: Harper & Row, 1982.

McGuire, Willliam and R. F. C. Hull, eds. *C. G. Jung Speaking: Interviews and Encounters.* Princeton, NJ: Princeton University Press, 1977.

Michael, Chester P. and Marie C. Norrisey. *Prayer and Temperament: Different Prayer Forms for Different Personality Types.* Charlottesville, VA: The Open Door, 1984.

Moore, Thomas. *Care of the Soul: A Guide for Cultivating Depth and Sacredness in Everyday Life.* New York: HarperCollins, 1992.

Myers, Isabel Briggs. "Interview." In Gordon Lawrence. *People Types and Tiger Stripes: A Practical Guide to Learning Styles.* 2d ed. Gainesville, FL: Center for Application of Psychological Type, 1982.

——, with Peter B. Myers. *Gifts Differing.* Palo Alto CA: Consulting Psychologists Press, 1980.

Oswald, Roy M. and Otto Kroeger. *Personality Type and Religious Leadership.* Washington, DC: The Alban Institute, Inc., 1988.

Page, Earl. *Looking at Type.* Gainesville, FL: Center for the Application of Psychological Type, 1983.

Sanford, John. *The Kingdom Within.* Philadelphia: J. B. Lippincott Company, 1970.

Schutz, William C. *The Interpersonal Underworld.* Palo Alto, CA: Science and Behavior Books, 1966.

——Schutz, William C. *Joy: Expanding Human Awareness.* New York: Grove Press, 1968.

Smith, Huston. *The Religions of Man.* New York: Harper & Row, 1958.

The State Newspaper. Columbia, SC, Monday, January 20, 1992.

Theophane, the Monk. *Tales of a Magic Monastery.* New York: Crossroad, 1981.

Turner, Nathan W. *Effective Leadership in Small Groups.* Valley Forge: Judson Press, 1977.

von Franz, Marie-Louise. *C. G. Jung: His Myth in Our Time.* New York: C. G. Jung Foundation for Analytical Psychology, 1975.

Whitemont, Edward C. *The Symbolic Quest: Basic Concepts of Analytic Psychology.* New York: Harper & Row, 1969.

Wilmer, Harry A., M.D. *Practical Jung: Nuts and Bolts of Jungian Psychotherapy.* Wilmette, IL: Chiron Publications, 1987.

The Alban Institute:
an invitation to membership

The Alban Institute, begun in 1979, believes that the congregation is essential to the task of equipping the people of God to minister in the church and the world. A multi-denominational membership organization, the Institute provides on-site training, educational programs, consulting, research, and publishing for hundreds of churches across the country.

The Alban Institute invites you to be a member of this partnership of laity, clergy, and executives—a partnership that brings together people who are raising important questions about congregational life and people who are trying new solutions, making new discoveries, finding a new way of getting clear about the task of ministry. The Institute exists to provide you with the kinds of information and resources you need to support your ministries.

Join us now and enjoy these benefits:

CONGREGATIONS, The Alban Journal, a highly respected journal published six times a year, to keep you up to date on current issues and trends.

Inside Information, Alban's quarterly newsletter, keeps you informed about research and other happenings around Alban. Available to members only.

Publications Discounts:

- ☐ 15% for Individual, Retired Clergy, and Seminarian Members
- ☐ 25% for Congregational Members
- ☐ 40% for Judicatory and Seminary Executive Members

Discounts on Training and Education Events

Write our Membership Department at the address below or call us at (202) 244-7320 for more information about how to join The Alban Institute's growing membership, particularly about Congregational Membership in which 12 designated persons receive all benefits of membership.

The Alban Institute, Inc.
4125 Nebraska Avenue, NW
Washington, DC 20016